Busy Ant Maths

Homework Guide 3

Series Editor: Peter Clarke

Authors: Elizabeth Jurgensen, Jeanette Mumford, Sandra Roberts

William Collins' dream of knowledge for all began with the publication of his first book in 1819. A self-educated mill worker, he not only enriched millions of lives, but also founded a flourishing publishing house. Today, staying true to this spirit, Collins books are packed with inspiration, innovation and practical expertise. They place you at the centre of a world of possibility and give you exactly what you need to explore it.

Collins. Freedom to teach.

Published by Collins
An imprint of HarperCollins*Publishers*
77–85 Fulham Palace Road
Hammersmith
London
W6 8JB

Browse the complete Collins catalogue at
www.collins.co.uk

10 9 8 7 6 5 4 3 2

ISBN 978-0-00-756245-9

The authors assert their moral rights to be identified as the authors of this work

British Library Cataloguing in Publication Data
A Catalogue record for this publication is available from the British Library

Publishing Manager: Fiona McGlade
Managing Editor: Sarah Thomas
Project editors: Hamish Baxter and Leah Willey
Production: Rachel Weaver
Editors: Catherine Dakin, Donna Cole and Jean Rustean
Cover design and artwork: Amparo Barrera
Internal design concept: Amparo Barrera
Designed: Neil Adams, Grasshopper Design Company
Illustrations: Louise Forshaw, Eva Sassin, Gwyneth Williamson and Steven Woods

Printed and bound by Martins the Printers Ltd, Berwick-upon-Tweed

MIX
Paper from
responsible sources
FSC **FSC™ C007454**
www.fsc.org

FSC™ is a non-profit international organisation established to promote the responsible management of the world's forests. Products carrying the FSC label are independently certified to assure consumers that they come from forests that are managed to meet the social, economic and ecological needs of present and future generations, and other controlled sources.

Find out more about HarperCollins and the environment at
www.harpercollins.co.uk/green

Contents

Unit 1

Week 1: **Number – Number and place value**
Lesson 2: Ways to partition
Lesson 4: Make the larger number

Week 2: **Number – Addition and subtraction**
Lesson 1: 2-digit addition
Lesson 4: Mental addition and subtraction

Week 3: **Geometry – Properties of shape**
Lesson 1: Shapes about the home
Lesson 4: Patterns of 3-D shapes

Unit 2

Week 1: **Number – Multiplication and division, including Number and place value**
Lesson 3: All about 3s
Lesson 4: 2s, 3s, 5s and 10s

Week 2: **Number – Fractions**
Lesson 1: Fractions at home
Lesson 3: Fraction snakes

Week 3: **Measurement (mass)**
Lesson 1: Grocery grams
Lesson 3: What's for supper?

Unit 3

Week 1: **Number – Addition and subtraction**
Lesson 1: Missing number additions
Lesson 3: Adding 1s, 10s and 100s

Week 2: **Number – Addition and subtraction**
Lesson 1: Missing number subtractions
Lesson 3: Subtracting 1s, 10s and 100s

Week 3: **Geometry – Properties of shape**
Lesson 2: Investigating robot routes
Lesson 4: Check out the angles

Unit 4

Week 1: **Number – Multiplication and division, including Number and place value**
Lesson 1: Counting in 4s
Lesson 2: Using the key facts to find the 4 multiplication table

Week 2: **Number – Multiplication and division, including Number and place value**
Lesson 2: Using the key facts to find the 8 multiplication table
Lesson 4: All things 8: solving word problems

Week 3: **Measurement (time)**
Lesson 1: Right on time
Lesson 2: Puzzle time

Unit 5

Week 1: **Number – Number and place value**
Lesson 2: Make the larger number
Lesson 3: Making amounts of money

Week 2: **Number – Addition and subtraction, including Measurement (money)**
Lesson 1: The café
Lesson 3: Fruit stall

Week 3: **Geometry – Properties of shape**
Lesson 2: Make and match shapes
Lesson 3: Four-way fit

Unit 6

Week 1: **Number – Multiplication and division, including Number and place value**
Lesson 1: Counting in steps of 2, 4 and 8
Lesson 2: Halving to find division facts

Week 2: **Number – Fractions**
Lesson 2: First to 1
Lesson 4: Jump in quarters

Week 3: **Measurement (length)**
Lesson 1: Lengths and lines in centimetres
Lesson 2: Lines in circles

Unit 7

Week 1: **Number – Addition and subtraction**
    Lesson 2: Practising the column method for addition
    Lesson 4: Spinning addition

Week 2: **Number – Addition and subtraction, including Measurement (money)**
    Lesson 2: Practising the column method for subtraction
    Lesson 3: Spinning subtraction

Week 3: **Statistics**
    Lesson 1: Keeping a tally
    Lesson 3: Tins, packets and bags

Unit 8

Week 1: **Number – Multiplication and division, including Number and place value**
    Lesson 2: Revising multiplication facts
    Lesson 3: Revising division facts

Week 2: **Number – Fractions**
    Lesson 1: Making pizzas
    Lesson 3: Fraction snakes (2)

Week 3: **Measurement (perimeter)**
    Lesson 3: Perimeter search
    Lesson 4: Join up the rectangles

Unit 9

Week 1: **Number – Number and place value**
    Lesson 1: Raffle raffle
    Lesson 4: Secret numbers

Week 2: **Number – Addition and subtraction**
    Lesson 1: Mental jumps
    Lesson 3: Practising the column method for subtraction

Week 3: **Geometry – Properties of shape**
    Lesson 1: Capital letters
    Lesson 3: Pin board puzzles

Unit 10

Week 1: **Number – Multiplication and division**
    Lesson 1: Multiplication using partitioning
    Lesson 3: Multiplication: Introducing the expanded written method

Week 2: **Number – Fractions**
    Lesson 2: Home fractions
    Lesson 3: Fraction wall equivalents

Week 3: **Measurement (volume and capacity)**
    Lesson 3: Multiples of millilitres
    Lesson 4: Kitchen capacities

Unit 11

Week 1: **Number – Addition and subtraction, including Measurement (money)**
    Lesson 2: Meet my addition target
    Lesson 3: Finding change

Week 2: **Number – Addition and subtraction**
    Lesson 2: Meet my subtraction target
    Lesson 4: Jumping forwards and backwards

Week 3: **Measurement (time)**
    Lesson 3: Calendar patterns
    Lesson 4: Today's TV Guide

Unit 12

Week 1: **Number – Multiplication and division**
    Lesson 2: Multiplication: Introducing the formal written method
    Lesson 4: Solving problems

Week 2: **Number – Multiplication and division**
    Lesson 1: Division using partitioning
    Lesson 3: Division using the formal written method

Week 3: **Statistics**
    Lesson 1: Weather pictograms
    Lesson 4: Coins bar chart

Name: _____ Date: _____

Ways to partition

Partition 2-digit numbers

Challenge 1

Write two calculations for each number star below.

Challenge 2

Complete all the calculations for each number star.

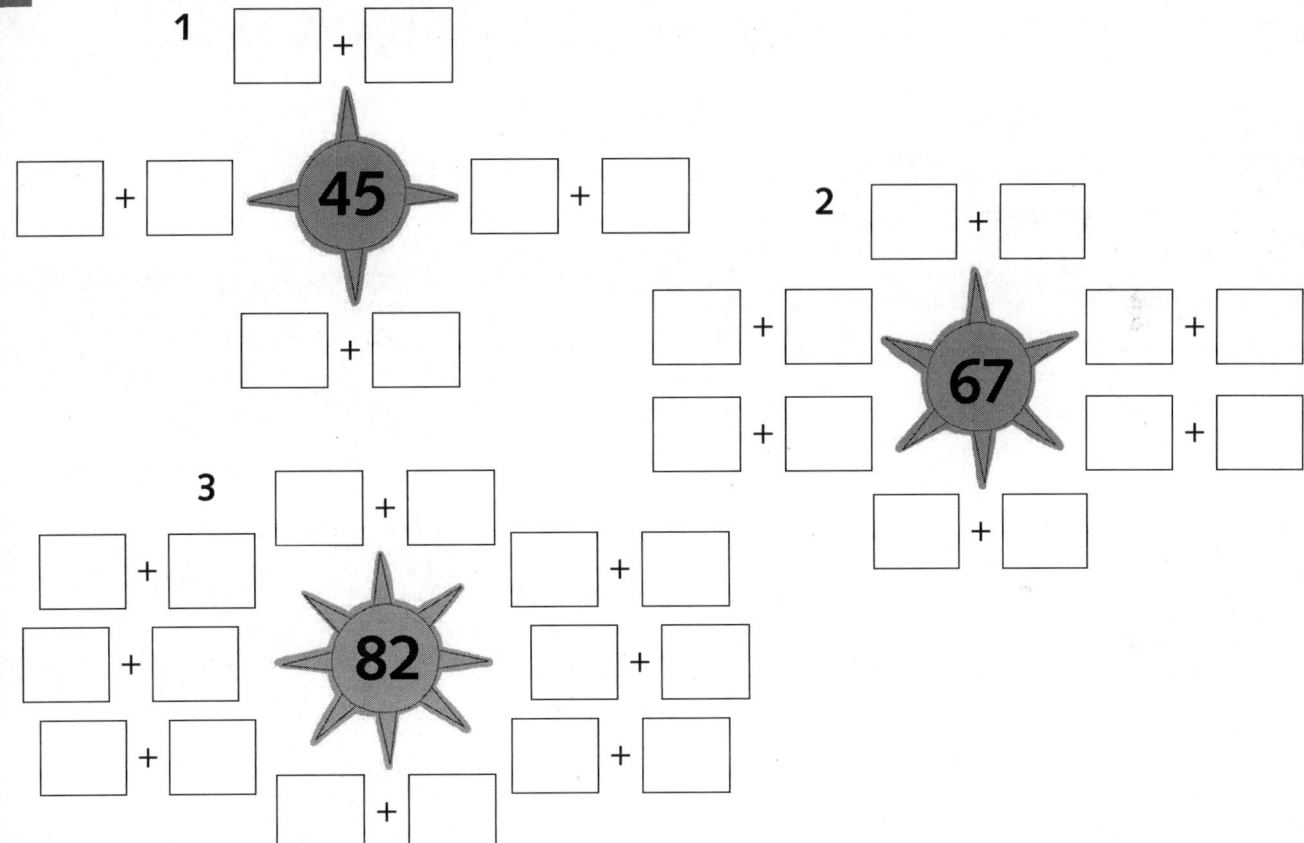

1 ☐ + ☐

☐ + ☐ **45** ☐ + ☐

☐ + ☐

2 ☐ + ☐

☐ + ☐ **67** ☐ + ☐

☐ + ☐   ☐ + ☐

☐ + ☐

3 ☐ + ☐

☐ + ☐   ☐ + ☐

☐ + ☐ **82** ☐ + ☐

☐ + ☐   ☐ + ☐

☐ + ☐

Challenge 3

Choose your own number to partition and complete all the calculations.
Then draw another number star on the back of this sheet.

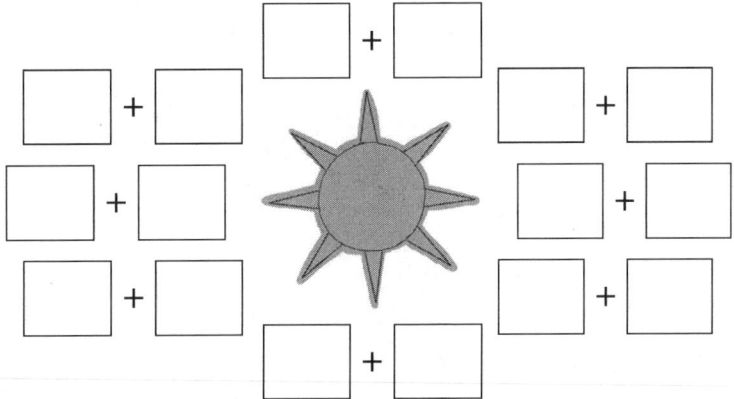

☐ + ☐

☐ + ☐   ☐ + ☐

☐ + ☐   ☐ + ☐

☐ + ☐   ☐ + ☐

☐ + ☐

 Ask an adult to suggest five 2-digit numbers. Together, partition them in
as many ways as you can. Write your answers on the back of this sheet.

Name: _____ Date: _____

Make the larger number

Compare numbers up to 1000

Challenge 1

Write the digits 1, 2, 3, 1, 2, 3
on the spinner.

Challenge 2

Write the digits 1–6 on the spinner.

Challenge 3

Write the digits 0, 4, 5, 7, 8 and 9
on the spinner.

You will need:
- paper clip and pencil
  – for the spinner

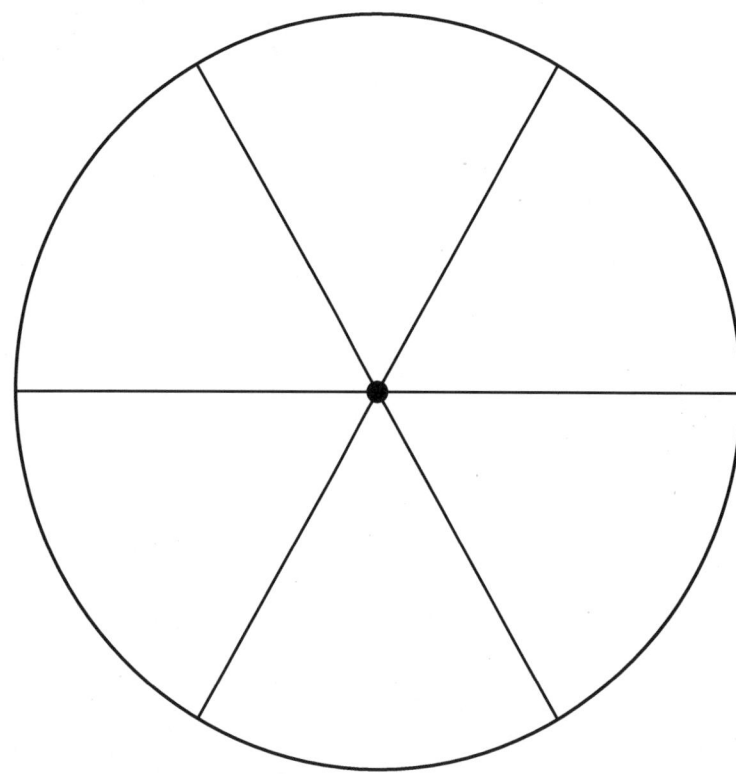

How to use the spinner
Hold the paper clip
in the centre of the
spinner using the
pencil, and gently flick
the paper clip with your
finger to make it spin.

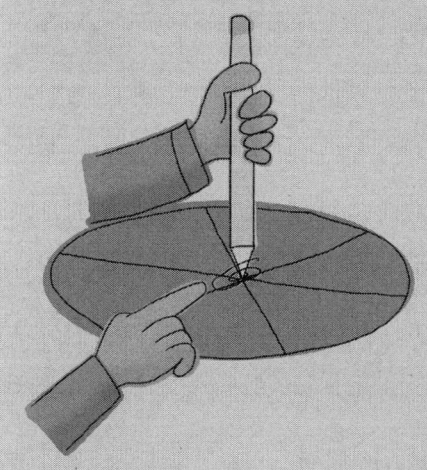

 Play this game with a partner.

- Each player should:
  - spin the spinner three times
  - use the digits to make a 3-digit number
  - say the number and write it down on the back of this sheet.

- The player with the larger number scores a point.

- The winner is the first player to score 10 points.

Name: _____ Date: _____

2-digit addition

Add two 2-digit numbers mentally

Choose from these numbers and make up ten addition calculations. Write them out below.

Example   23 + 16 = 39

14   24   21   16   23   13   15   22

Choose from these numbers and make up ten addition calculations. Write them out below.

Example   55 + 38 = 93

38   55   23   48   74   34   63   41

Choose from these numbers and make up ten missing number calculations below. Choose one number for the answer and a lower number to start the calculation. Work out the missing number.

Example   65 + 28 = 93

83   98   71   87   65   93   75   66

1 ____ + ____ = ____   2 ____ + ____ = ____

3 ____ + ____ = ____   4 ____ + ____ = ____

5 ____ + ____ = ____   6 ____ + ____ = ____

7 ____ + ____ = ____   8 ____ + ____ = ____

9 ____ + ____ = ____   10 ____ + ____ = ____

 Explain to someone at home how you add 2-digit numbers together.

Then, on the back of this sheet, write four calculations for them to work out using your method.

Name: _____ **Date:** _____

Mental addition and subtraction

Add and subtract numbers mentally

Challenge 1

a 61 + 6 = ☐

b 57 + 7 = ☐

c 82 + 5 = ☐

d 56 + 40 = ☐

e 68 + 30 = ☐

f 46 – 5 = ☐

g 31 – 6 = ☐

h 57 – 4 = ☐

i 69 – 20 = ☐

j 72 – 40 = ☐

Challenge 2

a 143 + 6 = ☐

b 286 + 7 = ☐

c 368 + 30 = ☐

d 387 + 70 = ☐

e 492 + 60 = ☐

f 229 – 7 = ☐

g 281 – 6 = ☐

h 386 – 50 = ☐

i 413 – 40 = ☐

j 532 – 60 = ☐

Challenge 3

a 428 + 7 = ☐

b 539 + 9 = ☐

c 683 + 70 = ☐

d 791 + 80 = ☐

e 865 + 50 = ☐

f 376 – 9 = ☐

g 781 – 5 = ☐

h 634 – 50 = ☐

i 812 – 70 = ☐

j 903 – 60 = ☐

 Choose one type of calculation, such as a 3-digit number add 10s. Explain to someone at home how to work out the answer. Then, on the back of this sheet, write four calculations for them to work out using your method.

Name: _____ Date: _____

Shapes about the home

Recognise 3-D shapes in any position

Find objects in your home that have these bases.

Write the name of the object in the table. Two are done for you.

Circular	Square	Rectangular
tin of beans		packet of cereal

1 Find about 12 different containers in your home. Arrange them into three sets according to the shape of their base.

2 Complete the table.

3 Circle the objects that are prisms.

Shape of base	Objects
Circular	
Square	
Rectangular	

There are different types of container in your kitchen: jar, bottle, box, packet and tin. Write your answers on the back of this sheet.

1 What shape of base do most cardboard containers have? Why do you think this is?

2 What shape of base do most tins have? Can you think why this is?

Find two different empty cardboard containers. Open each container and lay them flat to reveal the faces.

Discuss and compare the shape and size of the faces of each container.

Name: _____ Date: _____

Patterns of 3-D shapes

Build 3-D shapes with cubes

Challenge 1

1 Count the number of cubes in each cuboid and write your answers in the table below.

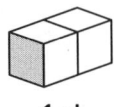 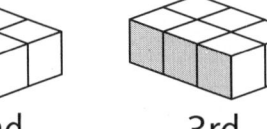 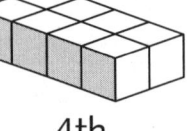 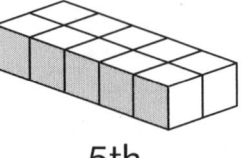

1st   2nd   3rd   4th   5th

2 How many cubes do you need for the 6th model?

Model	1st	2nd	3rd	4th	5th	6th
Number of cubes	2					

Challenges 2,3

1 Draw the 4th model in this row of cubes.

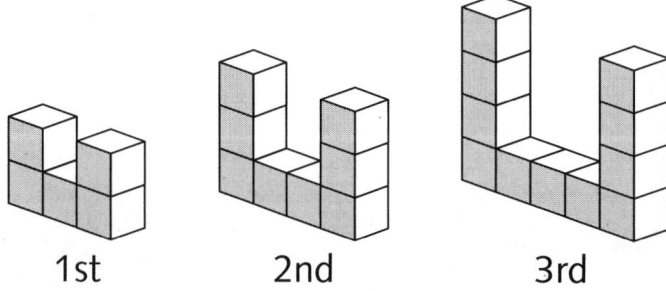

1st   2nd   3rd   4th

2 Count the number of cubes in each model and write your answers in the table below.

3 How many cubes do you need for the 5th and 6th models?

Model	1st	2nd	3rd	4th	5th	6th
Number of cubes	5					

Challenge 3

Look at the table of results for Challenges 2,3.
How many cubes would you need for the 10th model? [ ]

1 Using the bricks, work together to design and build your own pattern of 4 models.

You will need:
• building bricks

2 Discuss how you could use the pattern to make the 5th, 6th or even the 10th model.

Name: _____ Date: _____

All about 3s

Recall the multiplication and division facts for the 3 multiplication table

Challenge 1

Find the missing number in each multiplication and division trio.

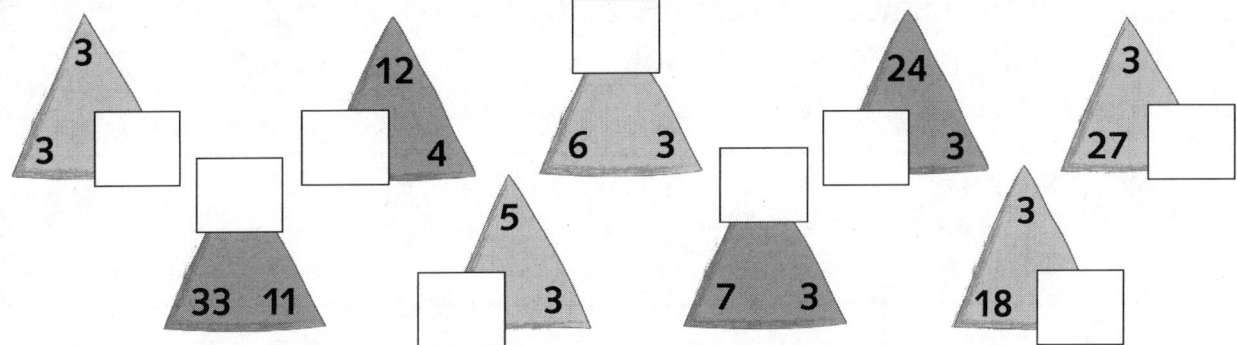

Challenge 2

Find the missing numbers.

a 8 × ☐ = 24

b 6 × ☐ = 30

c ☐ × 3 = 9

d 4 × ☐ = 20

e 10 × ☐ = 70

f ☐ × 3 = 33

g 9 × ☐ = 27

h 7 × ☐ = 21

i ☐ × 3 = 12

j 7 × ☐ = 14

k ☐ × 3 = 15

l 18 = ☐ × 3

m 5 × ☐ = 55

n 24 = ☐ × 3

o ☐ × 3 = 36

Challenge 3

Choose three trios from Challenge 1. Write the two multiplication and two division facts for each one.

Trio 1	Trio 2	Trio 3

 Once you have completed Challenge 2, ask an adult to read each question to you. See if you can remember the answers to each of the facts. Try to answer as quickly as you can!

Name: _____ Date: _____

2s, 3s, 5s and 10s

Recall the 2, 3, 5 and 10 multiplication tables and use these to solve problems

Challenge 1

Cross out the number in each row that is not in the multiplication family of numbers, e.g. 33. Write a multiplication fact for each set of numbers.

Example 6 × 5 = 30

6	~~33~~	5	30	6 × 5 = 30
3	8	48	24	
7	42	35	5	
6	10	30	60	

Challenge 2

Divide each set of numbers by the number shown.

1   ÷5

25	
50	
15	

2   ÷2

14	
10	
18	

3   ÷3

15	
30	
21	

Challenge 3

Write the calculation and answer for each word problem on the back of this sheet.

a Each pizza will be split into 5 slices. How many slices are there in 3 pizzas?

b There are 24 flowers and 3 vases. The same number of flowers are put into each vase. How many are in each vase?

c There are 12 cakes on the plate. 3 are eaten. How many are left?

d Anna has 7 times more stamps than Jimmy. Jimmy has 3 stamps. How many stamps does Anna have?

Find some things in your house that come in groups of 2, 3, 5 or 10. Draw or write about them on the back of this sheet.

Name: _____ Date: _____

Fractions at home

Identify fractions of shapes and objects

Look around your house.
What fractions can you see?

Windows are good to look at.
What about your shelves?

Draw what you see on the back
of this sheet and write the
fraction below it.

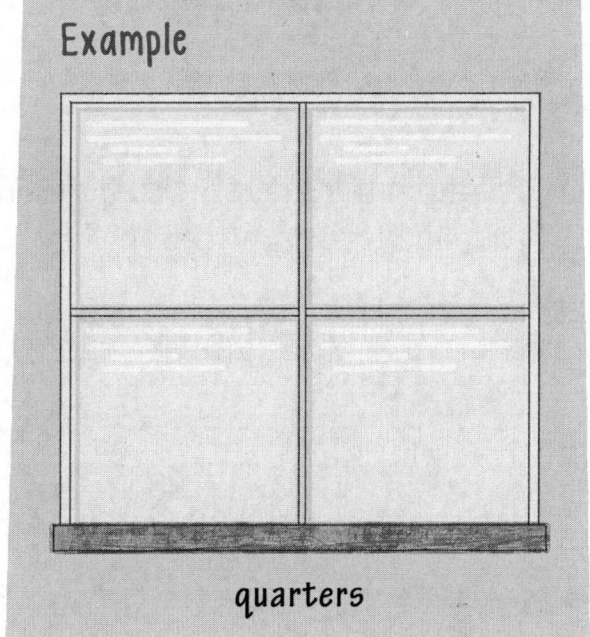

Example

quarters

Challenge 1

In your house, find as many halves as you can.

Challenge 2

In your house, find as many quarters as you can.

Challenge 3

In your house, can you find any thirds or fifths? Or any other fractions?

 Show your fractions to someone at home.

1 Explain to them what fraction each drawing is showing.

2 Ask them if they can find any other fractions.

Name: _____ Date: _____

Fraction snakes

Find fractions of amounts

You will need:
• coloured pencils

Colour in the snakes. Use different colours for each one. Write about your snakes using fractions.

Example 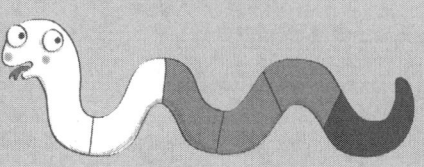   My snake is made of
$\frac{2}{6}$ white, $\frac{3}{6}$ grey and $\frac{1}{6}$ black .

Challenge 1

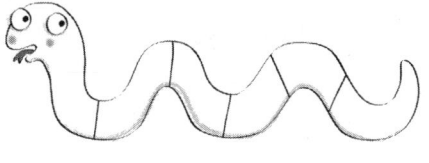

My snake is made of

.

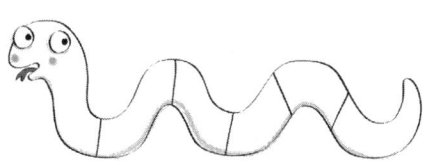

My snake is made of

.

Challenge 2

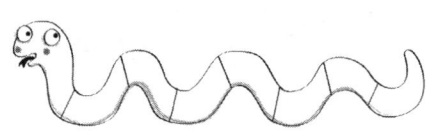

My snake is made of

.

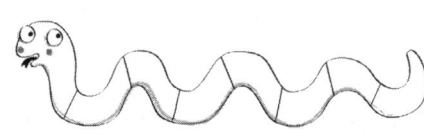

My snake is made of

.

Challenge 3

My snake is made of

.

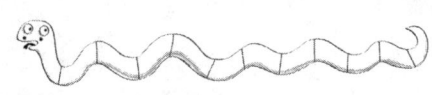

My snake is made of

.

 Show your snakes to someone at home and describe the fractions to them.

Name: _____ Date: _____

Grocery grams

Know $\frac{1}{2}$, $\frac{1}{4}$, and $\frac{3}{4}$ of 1 kg in grams

Look for the weight label on packets, tins and jars.

Write the name and mass in grams of three items for each set.

Challenge 1

Less than $\frac{1}{2}$ kg		Between $\frac{1}{2}$ kg and 1 kg	
Tin of baked beans	424 g	Frozen oven chips	900 g
1		1	
2		2	
3		3	

Challenge 2

Less than $\frac{1}{4}$ kg		Between $\frac{1}{4}$ kg and $\frac{1}{2}$ kg	
Tin of tuna	160 g	Jar of jam	454 g
1		1	
2		2	
3		3	

Challenge 3

Weighs less than $\frac{1}{4}$ kg	Weighs between $\frac{1}{4}$ kg and $\frac{1}{2}$ kg	Weighs between $\frac{1}{2}$ kg and 1 kg
1	1	1
2	2	2
3	3	3

 Can you find some items that have a combined mass of about 2 kg?
Write your answers on the back of this sheet.

Name: _____ Date: _____

What's for supper?

Use scaling of quantities in grams

Challenge 1

This recipe makes 1 batch of 15 chocolate crispies. Complete the table for the ingredients you need for 2 and 4 batches.

Ingredients	1 batch	2 batches	4 batches
Chocolate	100 g		
Margarine	25 g		
Cornflakes	150 g		
Honey	50 g		

Challenge 2

This recipe for Singapore rice noodles serves 2 people. Complete the table for the ingredients you need for 4, 8 and 10 people.

Ingredients	2 people	4 people	8 people	10 people
Rice noodles	100 g			
Cooked chicken	50 g			
Prawns	60 g			
Beansprouts	150 g			

Challenge 3

This Thai salad serves 4 people. Complete the table for the ingredients to serve 8, 10 and 5 people.

Ingredients	4 people	8 people	10 people	5 people
Sugar snap peas	150 g			
Rice noodles	250 g			
Cashew nuts	100 g			
Carrots	300 g			
Beansprouts	400 g			

Find a simple recipe in a book or online. Change the quantities for different numbers of people. Write your list of ingredients and their quantities on the back of this sheet.

Name: _____ Date: _____

Missing number additions

Add mentally, a 3-digit number and 1s

Work out these calculations mentally by finding the missing numbers.

Challenge 1

a 137 + 6 = ☐

b 145 + 7 = ☐

c 128 + 5 = ☐

d 161 + 7 = ☐

e 159 + 3 = ☐

f 166 + 6 = ☐

g 187 + 9 = ☐

h 199 + 8 = ☐

Challenge 2

a 246 + ☐ = 251

b 267 + ☐ = 275

c 208 + ☐ = 216

d 284 + ☐ = 291

e 295 + ☐ = 301

f 306 + ☐ = 313

g 343 + ☐ = 350

h 387 + ☐ = 392

Challenge 3

a 784 + ☐ = 793

b 759 + ☐ = 765

c 788 + ☐ = 793

d 796 + ☐ = 804

e 811 + ☐ = 818

f 847 + ☐ = 851

g 868 + ☐ = 875

h 899 + ☐ = 906

 Explain to someone at home how to work out the answers to missing number calculations. On the back of this sheet, make up some calculations for them to work out.

Name: _____ **Date:** _____

Adding 1s, 10s and 100s

Add mentally a 3-digit number and 1s, 10s and 100s

Work out these calculations. Use the back of this sheet for your working out.

Challenge 1

a 124 + 5 = ☐ **b** 132 + 6 = ☐

c 145 + 8 = ☐ **d** 126 + 20 = ☐

e 131 + 30 = ☐ **f** 148 + 20 = ☐

g 153 + 30 = ☐ **h** 149 + 100 = ☐

i 261 + 200 = ☐ **j** 350 + 300 = ☐

Challenge 2

a 153 + 9 = ☐ **b** 263 + 30 = ☐

c 229 + 50 = ☐ **d** 347 + 200 = ☐

e 151 + 300 = ☐ **f** 472 + 8 = ☐

g 504 + 400 = ☐ **h** 471 + 60 = ☐

i 293 + 9 = ☐ **j** 527 + 80 = ☐

Challenge 3

a 285 + ☐ = 315 **b** 379 + ☐ = 385

c 421 + ☐ = 721 **d** 736 + ☐ = 806

e 327 + ☐ = 927 **f** 597 + ☐ = 603

g 304 + ☐ = 803 **h** 299 + ☐ = 349

i 728 + ☐ = 808 **j** 444 + ☐ = 944

 Write a calculation – similar to the ones you have been working out – for someone at home. Teach them how to work it out.

Name: _____ Date: _____

Missing number subtractions

Subtract mentally, a 3-digit number and 1s

Work out these calculations mentally by finding the missing numbers.

Challenge 1

a 126 − 4 = ☐

b 134 − 3 = ☐

c 148 − 5 = ☐

d 151 − 5 = ☐

e 156 − 8 = ☐

f 164 − 7 = ☐

g 169 − 6 = ☐

h 177 − 9 = ☐

Challenge 2

a 367 − ☐ = 358

b 372 − ☐ = 368

c 381 − ☐ = 377

d 386 − ☐ = 379

e 394 − ☐ = 388

f 405 − ☐ = 396

g 413 − ☐ = 407

h 452 − ☐ = 445

Challenge 3

a 842 − ☐ = 835

b 815 − ☐ = 806

c 834 − ☐ = 828

d 847 − ☐ = 841

e 855 − ☐ = 847

f 882 − ☐ = 878

g 905 − ☐ = 897

h 914 − ☐ = 909

Explain to someone at home how to work out the answers to missing number calculations. On the back of this sheet, make up some calculations for them to work out.

Name: _____ Date: _____

Subtracting 1s, 10s and 100s

Subtract mentally a 3-digit number and 1s, 10s and 100s

Work out these calculations. Use the back of this sheet for your working out.

Challenge 1

a 128 – 6 = ☐   **b** 167 – 3 = ☐

c 177 – 6 = ☐   **d** 165 – 40 = ☐

e 179 – 30 = ☐   **f** 182 – 60 = ☐

g 197 – 50 = ☐   **h** 286 – 100 = ☐

i 291 – 100 = ☐   **j** 382 – 100 = ☐

Challenge 2

a 152 – 7 = ☐   **b** 283 – 6 = ☐

c 276 – 40 = ☐   **d** 325 – 60 = ☐

e 415 – 50 = ☐   **f** 587 – 70 = ☐

g 522 – 80 = ☐   **h** 583 – 300 = ☐

i 693 – 400 = ☐   **j** 799 – 500 = ☐

Challenge 3

a 296 – ☐ = 287   **b** 303 – ☐ = 298

c 451 – ☐ = 401   **d** 526 – ☐ = 476

e 635 – ☐ = 555   **f** 762 – ☐ = 692

g 859 – ☐ = 779   **h** 841 – ☐ = 141

i 952 – ☐ = 52   **j** 837 – ☐ = 237

 Write a calculation – similar to the ones you have been working out – for someone at home. Teach them how to work it out.

Name: _____ Date: _____

nvestigating robot routes

Make and describe right-angled turns

You will need:
• ruler

How many different routes can you navigate
from Start to Finish?

Challenge 1 Here is one route. Can you find another three?

Challenge 2 Can you find six different routes?

Challenge 3 Can you find all nine routes?

Example

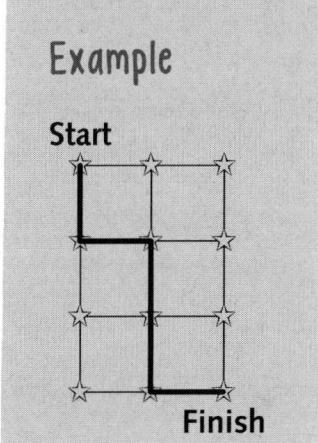

Start ... Finish

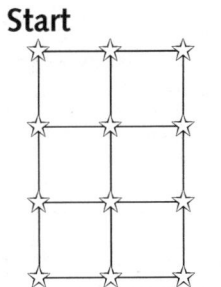

Start ... Finish

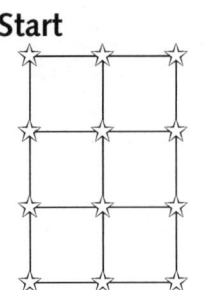

Start ... Finish

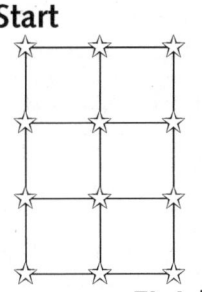

Start ... Finish

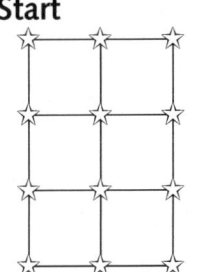

Start ... Finish

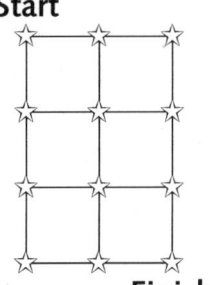

Start ... Finish

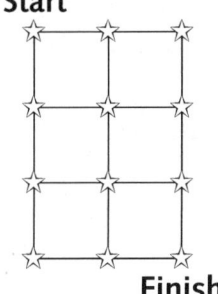

Start ... Finish

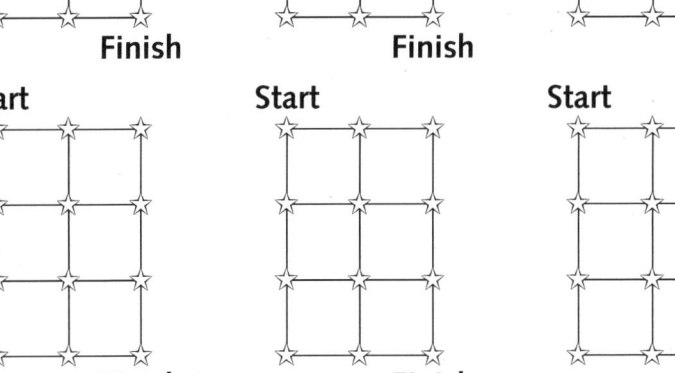

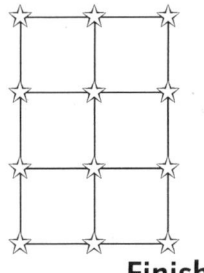

Start ... Finish

Think about routes you take at home, e.g. from your bedroom to the
kitchen. Write about and/or draw the routes on the back of this sheet
and show the number of right-angled turns you make.

Name: _____ Date: _____

Check out the angles

Test whether an angle is greater than or less than a right angle

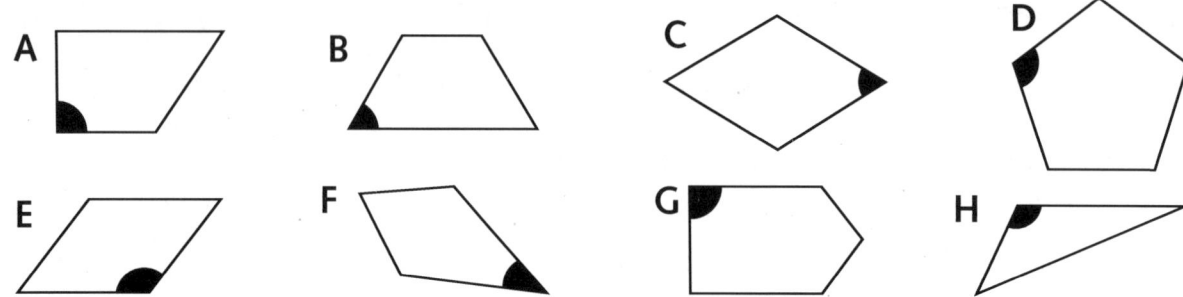

Challenges 1, 2

Look at the marked angle in each of the eight shapes. Write the letter of the shape in the correct row in the table.

Angle is less than a right angle	
Angle is a right angle	
Angle is greater than a right angle	

Challenges 2, 3

Write the letter of the shapes that have:

a at least two angles less than a right angle.

b at least two angles greater than a right angle.

Challenge 3

Write the letter of the shapes that have:

a all angles greater than a right angle.

b two angles greater than a right angle and two angles less than a right angle.

 Use a 50p coin and a 20p coin. How many angles greater than a right angle does each coin have? Write your answer on the back of this sheet.

Name: _____ Date: _____

Counting in 4s

Count in steps and multiples of 4

You will need:
• coloured pencils

Challenge 1

Write the multiples of 4 from 4 to 48.

4, ☐ , ☐ , ☐ , ☐ , ☐ , ☐ , ☐ , ☐ , ☐ , ☐ , 48

Challenge 2

1 Write the multiple of 4 that comes before these numbers.

a 24 ☐   b 8 ☐   c 16 ☐

d 36 ☐   e 40 ☐   f 12 ☐

2 Write the multiple of 4 that comes after these numbers.

a 44 ☐   b 32 ☐   c 20 ☐

d 12 ☐   e 24 ☐   f 8 ☐

Challenge 3

1 a Find and colour the multiples of 2.

(35) (24) (47) (15) (12) (8) (26) (25) (32) (3) (6) (17) (30) (4)

b Write the multiples of 2 in order, from smallest to largest.

☐

2 a Find and colour the multiples of 4.

(28) (14) (34) (4) (24) (12) (22) (32) (42) (8) (18) (16) (26) (36)

b Write the multiples of 4 in order, from smallest to largest.

☐

3 Are there any numbers that appear in both of your lists? Why is this?

_____

Look for multiples of 4 all around you – at home and when you're out and about. On the back of this sheet, draw or write at least four examples of multiples of 4 you have found, and record where you found them.

Name: _____ Date: _____

Using the key facts to find the 4 multiplication table

Recall the multiplication and division facts for the 4 multiplication table

Find the missing number in each multiplication and division trio.

1 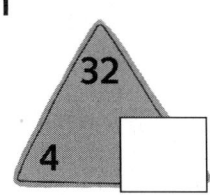 2 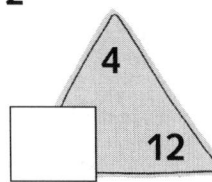 3 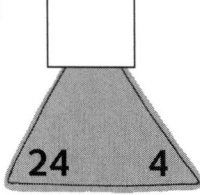 4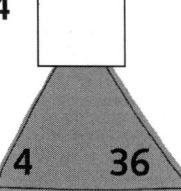

5 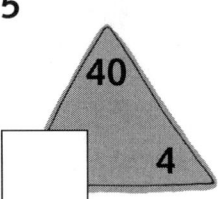 6 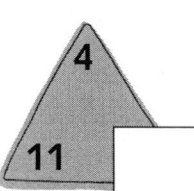 7 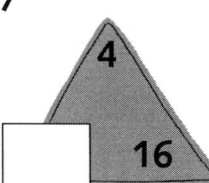 8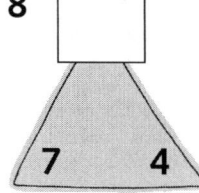

1 8 × ☐ = 32   2 6 x 4 = ☐   3 ☐ × 4 = 36

4 4 × ☐ = 20   5 40 ÷ 4 = ☐   6 ☐ × 4 = 44

7 36 ÷ ☐ = 4   8 7 × ☐ = 28   9 ☐ × 3 = 12

Choose three trios from Challenge 1. Write the two multiplication and two division facts for each one.

Trio 1	Trio 2	Trio 3

 Once you have completed Challenge 2, ask an adult to read each question to you. See if you can remember the answers to each of the facts. Try to answer as quickly as you can!

Name: _____ Date: _____

Using the key facts to find the 8 multiplication table

Recall the multiplication and division facts for the 8 multiplication table

1 Write the first 12 multiples of 8 in the boxes below.

2 Circle the multiples boxes above that relate to the key facts for the 8 multiplication table.

Use the key facts to work out the answers to these multiplication facts. Write in the thought bubble which key fact helped you to work out the answer.

3 × 8 = ☐   7 × 8 = ☐

12 × 8 = ☐   9 × 8 = ☐

4 × 8 = ☐   8 × 8 = ☐

11 × 8 = ☐   6 × 8 = ☐

Write a multiplication fact (× 8) and division fact (÷ 8) for each array.

1 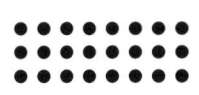   **2** 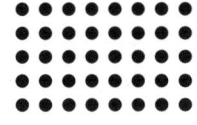   **3**

 Ask an adult to say a multiple of 8. Start from that number and keep counting in 8s until you reach 96. Repeat using different multiples of 8.

Name: _____ Date: _____

All things 8: solving word problems

Solve word problems

 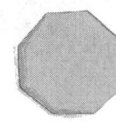  

Challenge 1

Write the calculation and answer to these questions about 8s.

Example $2 \times 8 = 16$

a 7 spiders. How many legs?

b 4 rowing boats. How many oars?

c 9 octopuses. How many legs?

d 6 octagons. How many sides?

e 5 tug of war matches.
How many people altogether?

Challenge 2

Write the calculation and answer to these questions about 8s.

Example $16 \div 2 = 8$

a 64 spider legs. How many spiders?

b 32 octopus legs. How many octopuses?

c 32 sides. How many octagons? How many squares? How many triangles?

d 28 people. Can 4 teams be made?
If not, how many teams can be made?

Challenge 3

 Make up some questions of your own about 8s. Write the calculation and answer on the back of this sheet.

 Look for multiples of 8 all around you – at home and when you're out and about. On the back of this sheet, draw or write at least four examples of multiples of 8 you found and where.

Name: _____ **Date:** _____

Right on time

Tell and write the time to the minute on a 12-hour clock with hands

Example

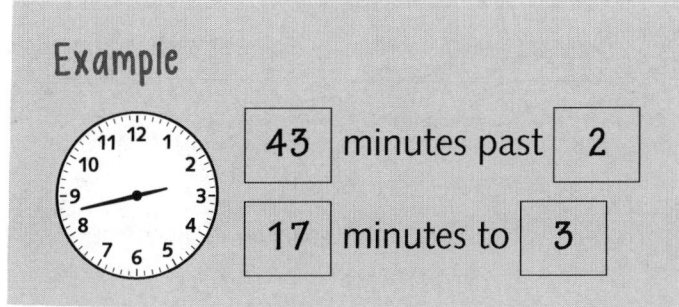

| 43 | minutes past | 2 |

| 17 | minutes to | 3 |

Challenge 1

Write these times in two ways.

1  ☐ minutes past ☐   ☐ minutes to ☐

2 ☐ minutes past ☐   ☐ minutes to ☐

Challenge 2

Each clock is either fast or slow.

Write what time each clock should show in two ways.

1  20 minutes slow

☐ minutes past ☐   ☐ minutes to ☐

2  10 minutes fast

☐ minutes past ☐   ☐ minutes to ☐

Challenge 3

These clock faces have been reflected in a mirror. Write the correct time for each clock.

1    **2**    **3**

☐   ☐   ☐

Working together, look at the TV listings and on the back of this sheet write down the times that 6 different programmes start. Write the times for each programme in two different ways.

Name: _____ Date: _____

Puzzle time

Use a time line and the vocabulary of time

Challenge 1

List four things you have done today in the boxes below. Draw an arrow to the time line for each item in your list.

a	b	c	d

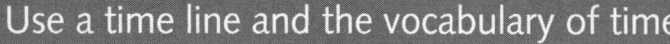

6 a.m.   9 a.m.   12 noon   6 p.m.

Challenge 2

Andy drew this time line of his journey to Spain.

6 a.m.   12 noon   6 p.m.

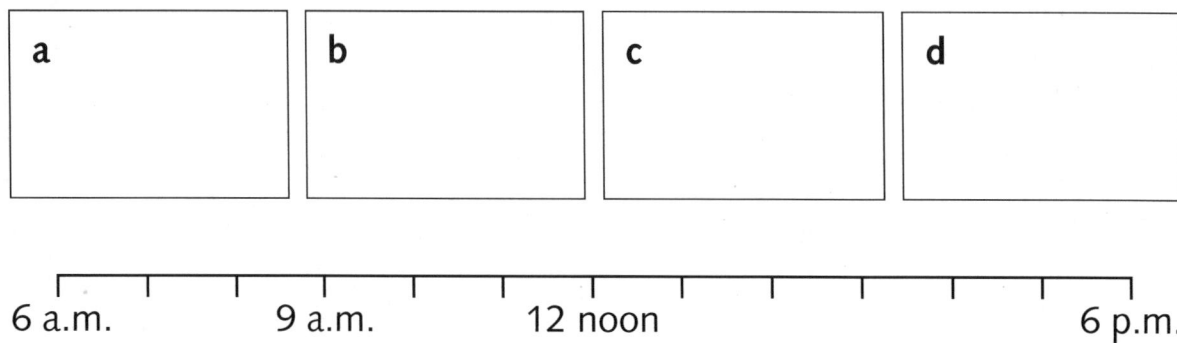

Get up Taxi to   Flight   Flight Arrive In the
         airport   departs   lands   hotel   pool

1 Write the time under each arrow as an a.m. or p.m. time.

2 How many minutes before noon did his flight depart? [ ] minutes

3 How long did it take Andy from arriving at the hotel to getting in the pool?

Challenge 3

You must boil two eggs. One should be hard-boiled for 7 minutes and one should be soft-boiled for 4 minutes. Both eggs must be ready at exactly the same time. You have two egg timers, one for 3 minutes and one for 5 minutes.

1 Using a time line, show how you will use them to time the eggs correctly.

2 On the other side of this sheet, show how you worked out the answer.

 Plan a family day out. Work together and draw a time line for that day.

Name: _____ **Date:** _____

Make the larger number

Compare and order numbers up to 1000

You will need:
- paper clip and pencil
  – for the spinner

Challenge 1

Write these numbers on your spinner: 10, 10, 1, 10, 1, 1.

Challenge 2

Write these numbers on your spinner: 100, 10, 1, 100, 10, 1.

Challenge 3

Write these numbers on your spinner: 100, 10, 1, 100, 10, 1. Circle one each of the 100s, 10s and 1s. These are your bonus numbers. If you spin a bonus number you can double it.

How to use the spinner
Hold the paper clip in the centre of the spinner using the pencil and gently flick the paper clip with your finger to make it spin.

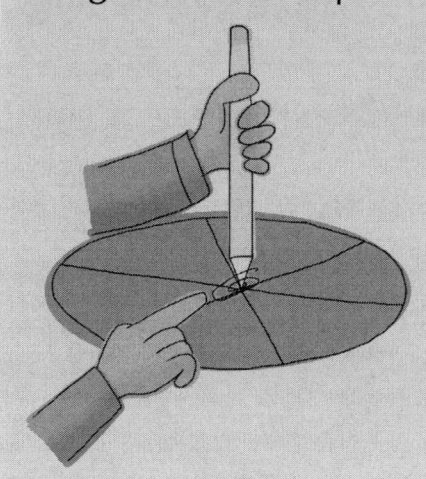

Play this game with a partner.

- Take turns to:
  – spin the spinner four times
  – write down the numbers that you spin
  – add them all together to make your number.

- The player with the larger number scores 1 point.

- The winner is the first player to win 10 points.

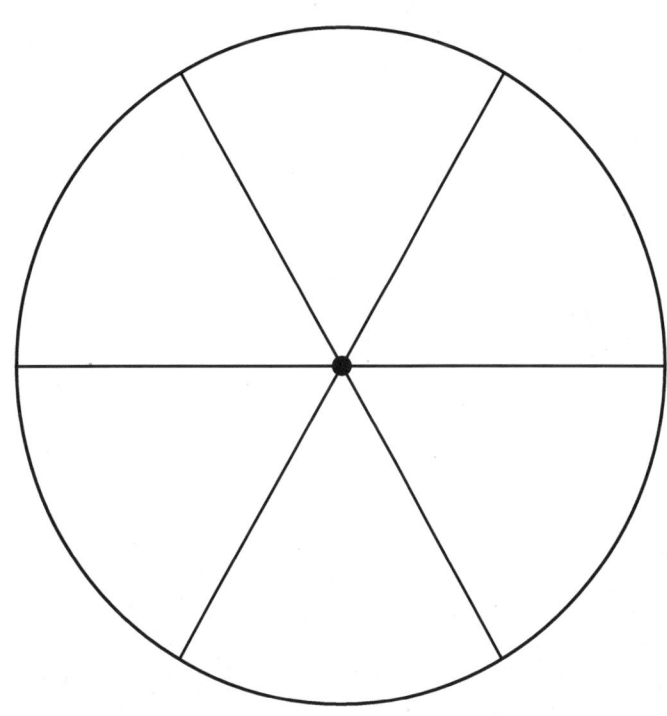

Name: _____ Date: _____

Making amounts of money

Represent and estimate numbers using money

Take some coins out of the bag, then draw the coins into a purse below. Count up the money in the purse and write the total amount in the answer box. Do this eight times.

 Challenge 1 Take 4 coins each time.

 Challenge 2 Take 6 coins each time.

 Challenge 3 Take 8 coins each time.

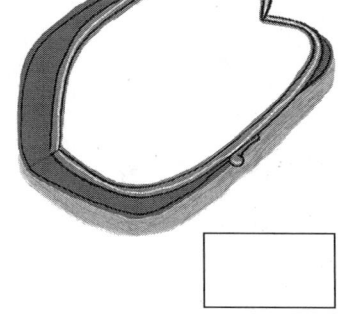 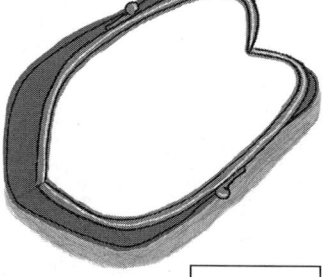

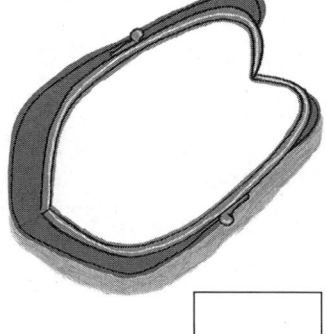 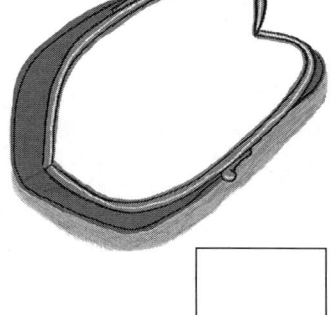 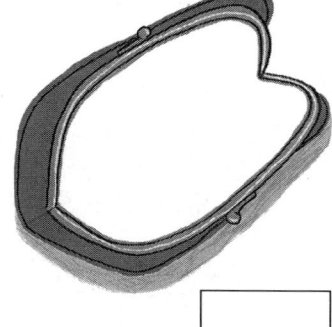

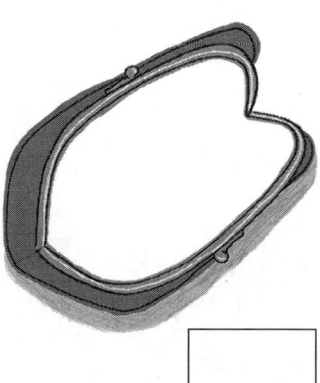 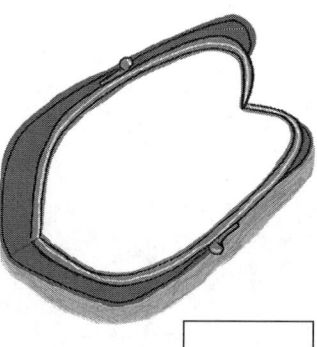 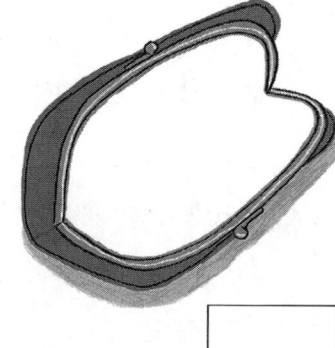

 Find someone to play with. Secretly take some coins out of the bag and count up the amount. Tell the other player the amount. Can they guess which coins you have in your hand? Now swap roles.

Name: _____ Date: _____

The café

Add amounts of money

Fill in the café menu with things you would like to eat and drink.
Write the price of each item.

Challenge 1

In your café, all food and drink costs less than 50p.

Challenge 2

In your café, all food and drink costs between 50p and £1.

Challenge 3

In your café, all food and drink costs between £1 and £2.

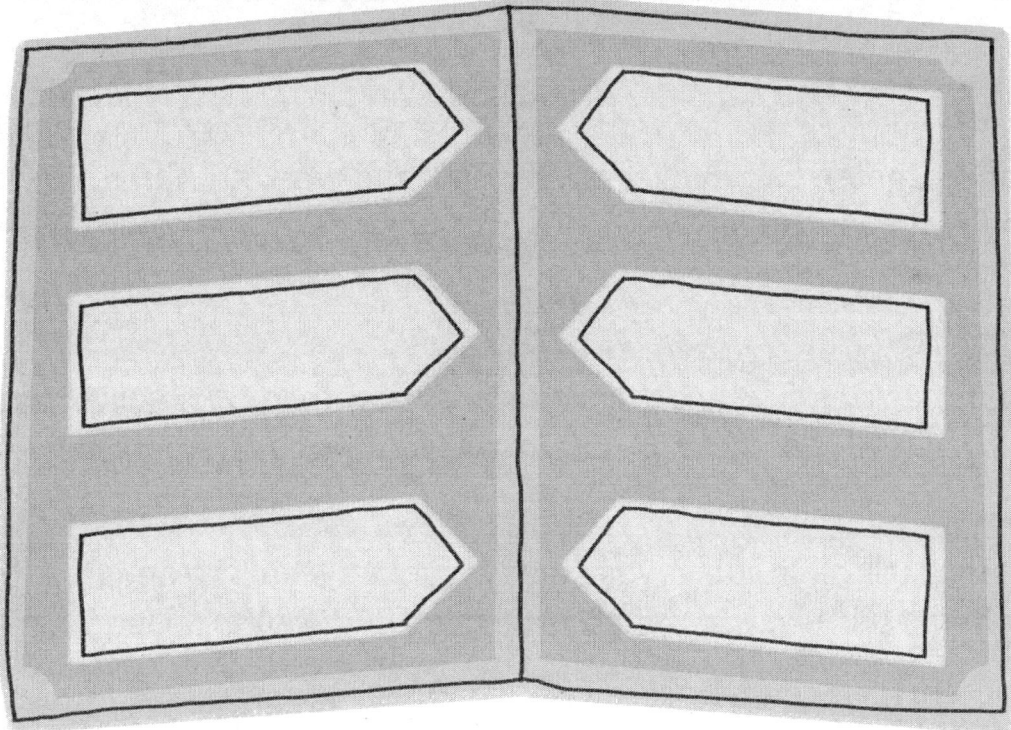

Choose two items from your café and work out how much they will cost.

Write your calculation on the back of this sheet. Repeat six times.

 Work with someone at home.

Take turns to:

• choose two items from the café menu

• add the prices together – mentally if you can.

Name: _____ Date: _____

Fruit stall

Add and subtract amounts of money

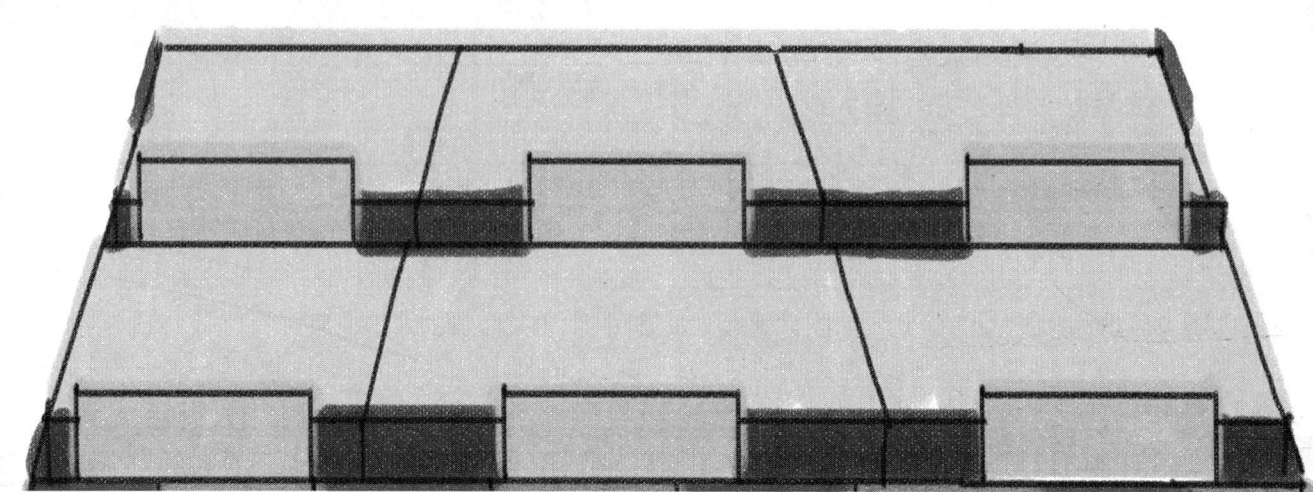

On the empty trays, draw the fruit or vegetables that you would like to buy. Choose two items from the stall and work out the cost. Then work out your change. Write your calculations on the back of this sheet. Repeat this six times.

Challenge 1

On the stall, all fruit and vegetables cost less than 50p. Write the price on each label. You have £1 (100p) to spend each time.

Challenge 2

On the stall, all fruit and vegetables cost between 50p and £1 (100p). Write the price on each label. You have £2 (200p) to spend each time.

Challenge 3

On the stall, all fruit and vegetables cost between £1 (100p) and £2 (200p). Write the price on each label. You have £5 (500p) to spend each time.

Ask someone at home to choose two items from the stall. Ask them to work out the total. Then ask them to work out the change from £1, £2 or £5. Repeat this four times.

Name: _____ Date: _____

Make and match shapes

Make shapes that match a property

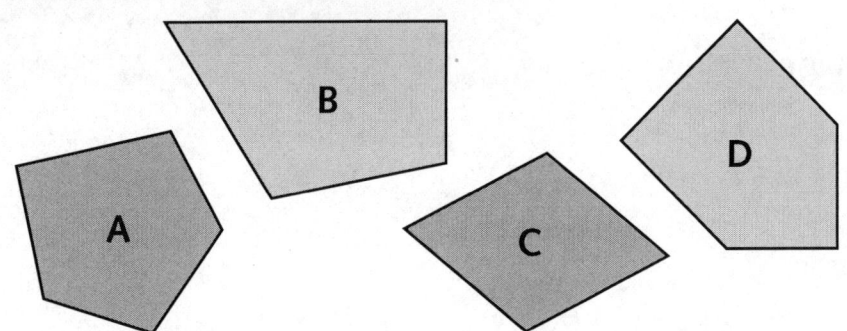

You will need:
- right-angle tester
- blue and red pencils

Find the shape above to match these properties.

Shape	4 sides	Sides same length
B	✓	✗
	✓	✓
	✗	✗

Shape	5 vertices	1 or more right angles
	✓	✓
	✗	✓
	✗	✗

Challenge 2

For shapes **A** to **F**:

- circle the right angles in red

- mark the equal sides (=) in blue.

Challenge 3

Look at shapes **B** and **F**. How are they alike? How are they different? Write your answers on the back of this sheet.

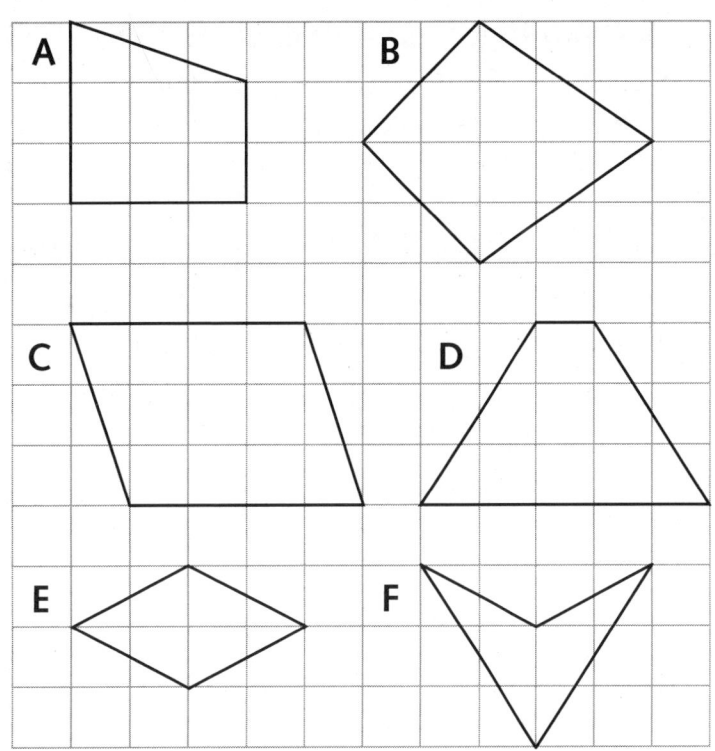

 Find out the collective name that we give all of the shapes **A** to **F**. _____

Name: _____ Date: _____

Four-way fit

Make shapes using folding and cutting

You will need:
- scissors
- coloured pencils
- ruler

Cut out the eight shapes below.

Use the four L-shapes.
Fit them on to this grid.
Use colour to show how the
shapes fit on to the grid.

Use the four T-shapes. Fit them on to
this grid. Use colour to show how the
shapes fit on to the grid.

Take four L-shapes and two T-shapes.
Fit them together to make a rectangle
4 units by 6 units. Draw your shape
on the back of this sheet.

 Make the following rectangles and draw them roughly on the back
of this sheet.
a The longest rectangle possible using all eight shapes.
b A rectangle 8 units by 3 units using four T-shapes and two L-shapes.

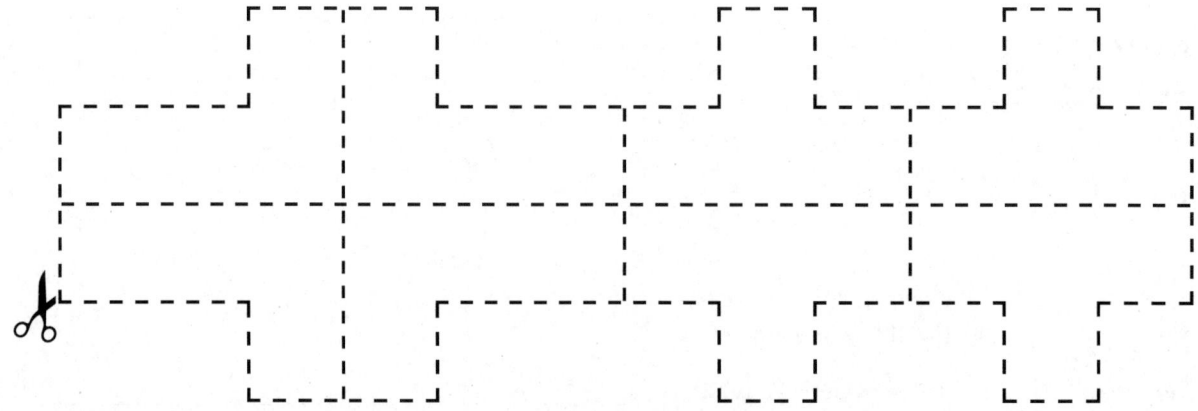

Name: _____ Date: _____

Counting in steps of 2, 4 and 8

Count in multiples of 2, 4 and 8

Challenge 1

Find and colour the multiples of each number.

2
(12) (32) (27) (16) (25) (43) (34) (61) (4) (13)

4
(16) (34) (24) (38) (28) (18) (10) (36) (42) (40)

8
(72) (56) (48) (12) (38) (62) (16) (45) (64) (90)

Challenge 2

Write the first 12 multiples of each number in order, from smallest to largest.

2 → [ ] [ ] [ ] [ ] [ ] [ ] [ ] [ ] [ ] [ ] [ ] [ ]

4 → [ ] [ ] [ ] [ ] [ ] [ ] [ ] [ ] [ ] [ ] [ ] [ ]

8 → [ ] [ ] [ ] [ ] [ ] [ ] [ ] [ ] [ ] [ ] [ ] [ ]

Challenge 3

Complete the grid.

x	3	9	6	10	8	5	7
2							
4						20	
8							

Count the different types of shoes in your home.
Write how many pairs of each shoe type you find in the table.
Place a tick in the correct multiples box.

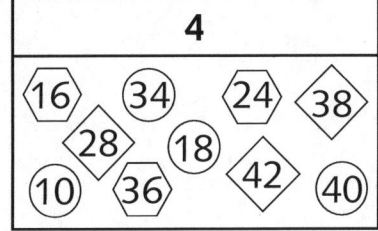

	Trainers	Women's high heels	Men's shoes	Women's flat shoes
	[ ]	[ ]	[ ]	[ ]
Multiple of 2				
Multiple of 4				
Multiple of 8				

Name: _____ Date: _____

Halving to find division facts

Use halving to recall the division facts for the 4 multiplication table

Challenge 1

Halve each number.

a 48 → ☐   b 24 → ☐   c 12 → ☐   d 20 → ☐

e 40 → ☐   f 32 → ☐   g 16 → ☐   h   8 → ☐

Challenge 2

Write the total number of stamps under each array. The post office worker sells half the stamps. Write how many are left. She sells half again. Write how many are left. Write a division fact for each array using the 4 multiplication table.

Example

$20 \div 4 = 5$

÷2   ÷2
| 20 | 10 | 5 |

1
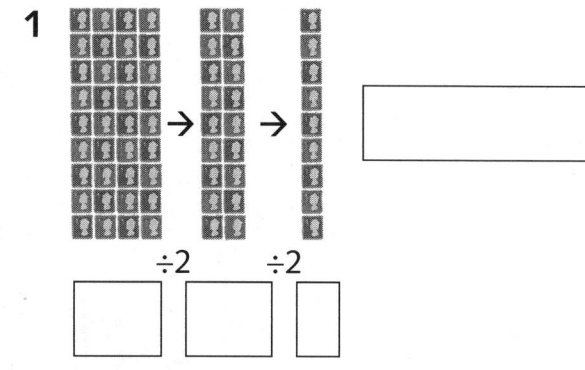

÷2   ÷2
☐ ☐ ☐

2
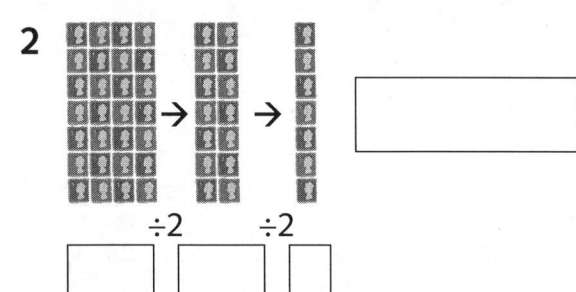

÷2   ÷2
☐ ☐ ☐

3
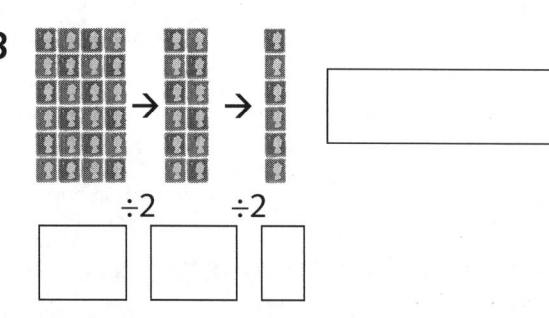

÷2   ÷2
☐ ☐ ☐

Challenge 3

Four children share some fruit. To find out how much they get, divide each bag by 4. Write the division fact.

1  24 ☐   2  28 ☐   3  32 ☐

 Ask an adult to say a multiple of 4 up to 48. Halve the number and then halve it again. Tell them your answer and check if you are correct. Swap roles. Check if their answer matches yours.

Name: _____ Date: _____

First to 1

Make and name fractions

- Take turns to:
  - spin the spinner
  - colour in that number of sections in your circle
  - say which fraction of your circle is shaded.

- The winner is the first player to colour their whole circle.

How to use the spinner
Hold the paper clip in the centre of the spinner using the pencil and gently flick the paper clip with your finger to make it spin.

Player 1   **Player 2**

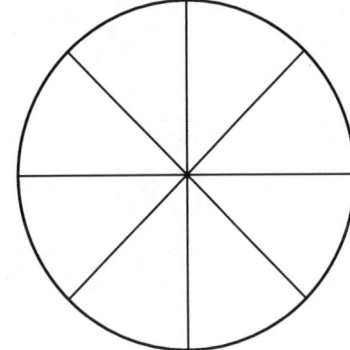   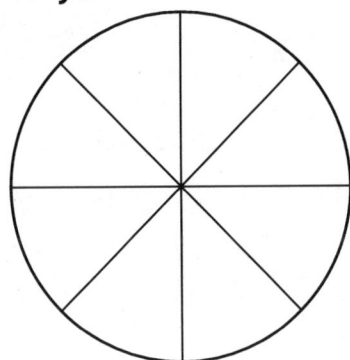

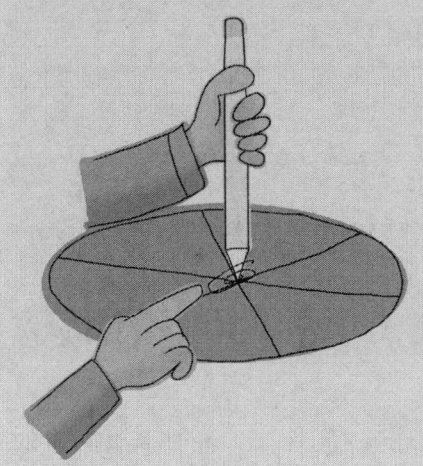

Challenge 1

Play the game as above.

Challenge 2

Play the game. After each turn, say how many more fractions you need to colour to win.

Challenge 3

How many sixteenths are the same as:

1 $\frac{1}{2}$ of the circle?

2 $\frac{1}{4}$ of the circle?

3 $\frac{1}{8}$ of the circle?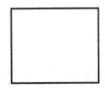

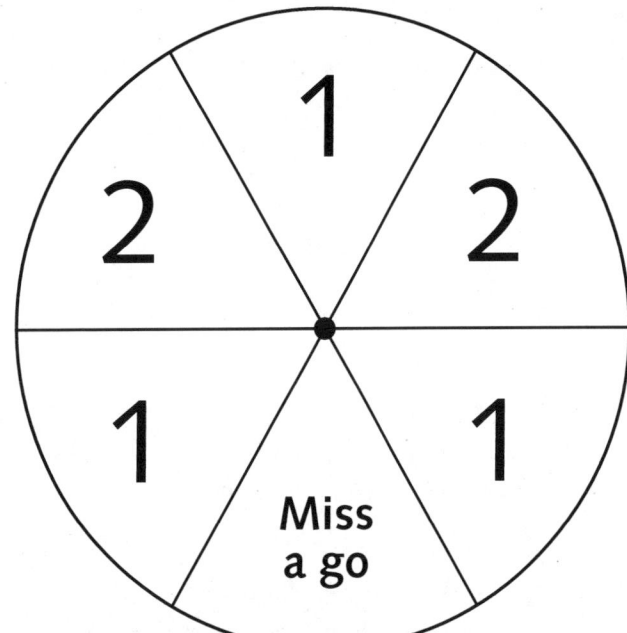

Name: _____ Date: _____

Jump in quarters

Recognise fractions as numbers

• Take turns to:
    – spin the spinner
    – read out the fraction it lands on
    – jump that many quarters on or back along the number line.

• The winner is the first player to land exactly on 3.

Player 1

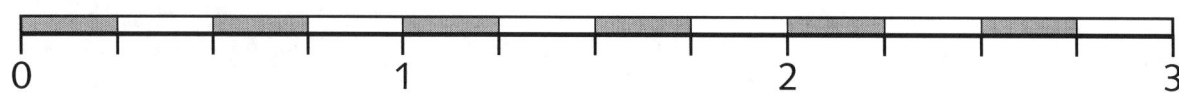

0   1   2   3

Player 2

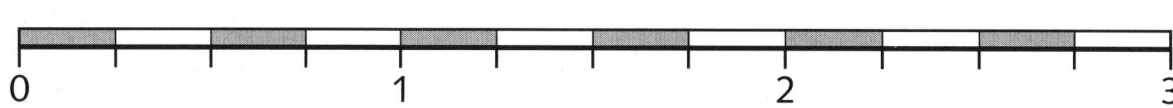

0   1   2   3

Challenge 1
Write these fractions on the spinner: $\frac{1}{4}, \frac{2}{4}, \frac{1}{4}, \frac{2}{4}$

Challenge 2
Write these fractions on the spinner: $+\frac{1}{4}, -\frac{2}{4}, +\frac{2}{4}, +\frac{3}{4}$
(You cannot jump back past zero.)

Challenge 3
Write these fractions on the spinner: $+\frac{1}{4}, -\frac{2}{4}, +\frac{2}{4}, +\frac{3}{4}$
(You cannot jump back past zero.)
After each move, say how many quarters you have moved altogether.

How to use the spinner
Hold the paper clip
in the centre of the
spinner using the pencil
and gently flick the
paper clip with your
finger to make it spin.

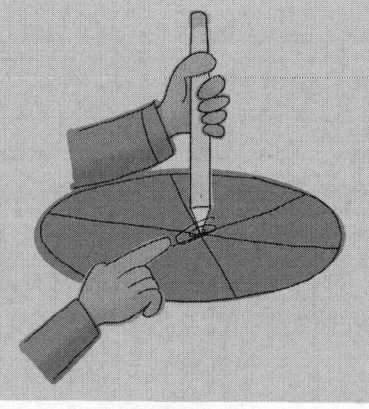

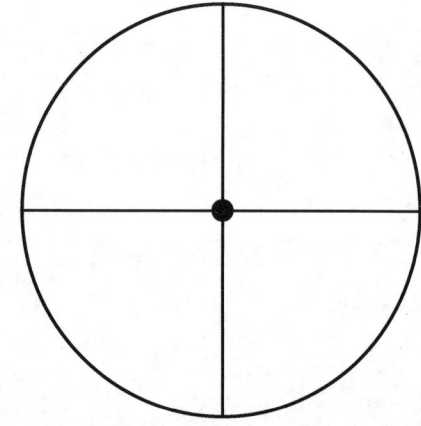

Name: _____ Date: _____

Lengths and lines in centimetres

Use a ruler to draw and measure lines to the nearest centimetre

Challenges 1,2,3

Measure the lines in the hexagon
to the nearest centimetre.

A to B = ☐ cm

A to C = ☐ cm

A to D = ☐ cm

A to E = ☐ cm

A to F = ☐ cm

You will need:
- ruler
- pencil

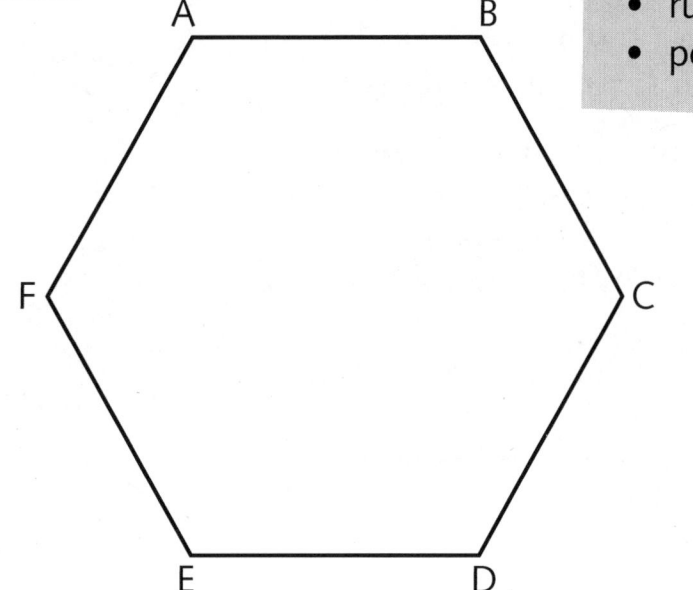

Challenges 2,3

Complete these statements.

1 Line AC is the same length as line ☐.

2 Line AD is twice as long as line ☐.

Challenge 3

☐ 1 cm

☐ 12 cm

☐ 3 cm

☐ 9 cm

You have these four rods. Can you use these rods to measure every
centimetre length from 1 cm to 25 cm?

Record your findings on the back of this sheet.

Choose an item at home of less than 30 cm. Each person estimates the
length of the item. Measure the item. The person whose estimate is the
closest wins one point. Repeat with different items. The first person to
5 points is the winner.

Name: _____ Date: _____

Lines in circles

Use a ruler to draw and measure lines
to the nearest millimetre

You will need:
- ruler
- coloured pencils

Challenges 1, 2, 3

1 Join these points with straight lines.
1 to 2, 1 to 3, 1 to 4, 1 to 5,
1 to 6, 1 to 7 and 1 to 8.

2 Measure each line to the nearest
millimetre. Complete the table.

Line	Length in mm
1 to 2	
1 to 3	
1 to 4	
1 to 5	
1 to 6	
1 to 7	
1 to 8	

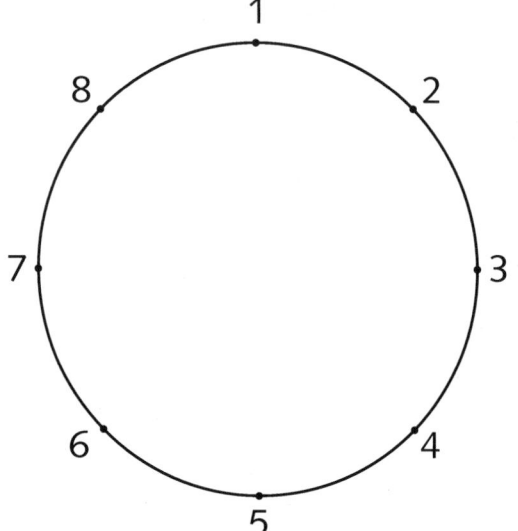

Measure from
the centre of
the dots.

Challenges 2, 3

Use the circle in Challenges 1, 2, 3. Join 2 to 3, 2 to 4, 2 to 5, 2 to 6,
2 to 7 and 2 to 8. Continue in this way to join points from one dot
to all the other dots.

Challenge 3

Look for a pattern made by the lines in the circle.
Rule all the lines that are the same length in the same colour.

Together with someone at home, look at the
shape formed by joining the points 2 to 4, 4 to 6,
6 to 8 and 8 to 1. Can you name this shape? _____

Look at the shape formed by joining the points
1 to 3, 3 to 5 and 5 to 1. How often is this shape
repeated in the pattern? _____

Name: _____ Date: _____

Practising the column method for addition

Add 3-digit numbers using the formal written method of column addition

Work out the answers to the calculations using the written method for addition. Show your working below.

Challenge 1

a 138 + 151   b 126 + 163   c 254 + 125   d 203 + 281

e 174 + 225   f 237 + 252   g 316 + 151   h 277 + 312

Challenge 2

a 267 + 312   b 281 + 316   c 423 + 352   d 306 + 481

e 521 + 355   f 347 + 328   g 419 + 326   h 258 + 424

Challenge 3

a 648 + 329   b 519 + 437   c 707 + 187   d 382 + 618

e 535 + 328   f 618 + 376   g 446 + 436   h 724 + 259

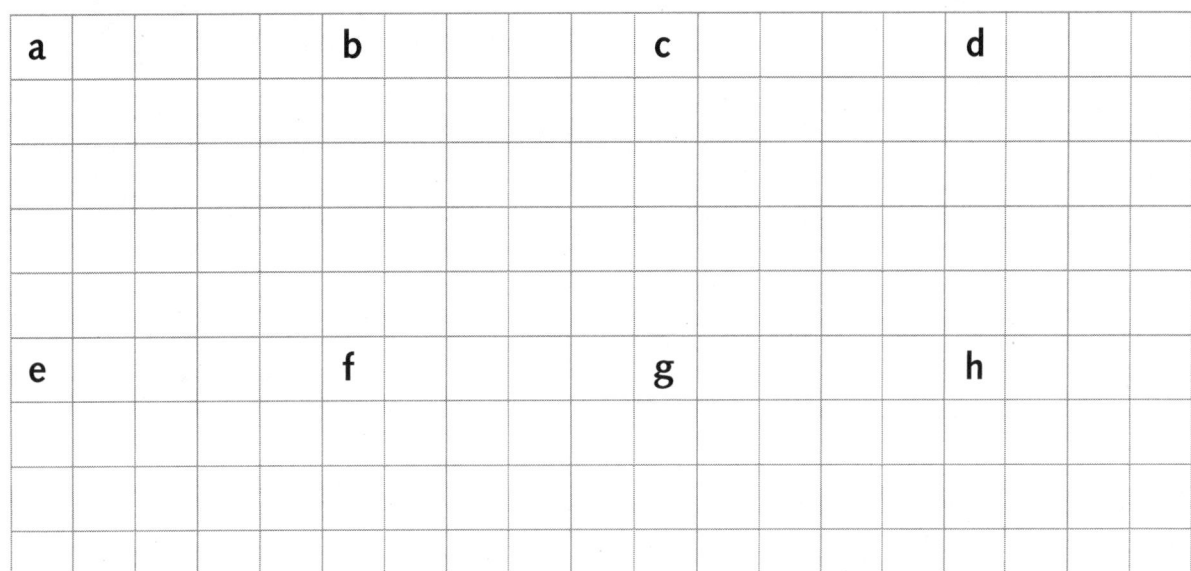

 Choose four of your calculations. Ask someone at home to work them out. Did you both get the same answers?

Name: _____ Date: _____

Spinning addition

Add numbers mentally and use inverse
operations to check the answer

You will need:
- paper clip and pencil
  – for the spinner

Challenge 1
Choose a first number between 10 and 99.

Challenge 2
Choose a first number between 100 and 400.

Challenge 3
Choose a first number between 400 and 600.

How to use the spinner
Hold the paper clip
in the centre of the
spinner using the pencil
and gently flick the
paper clip with your
finger to make it spin.

- Choose a number to write in the first box
  of the addition calculations below.

- Spin the spinner and write the number
  in the second box.

- Add the numbers together either mentally
  or using a number line.

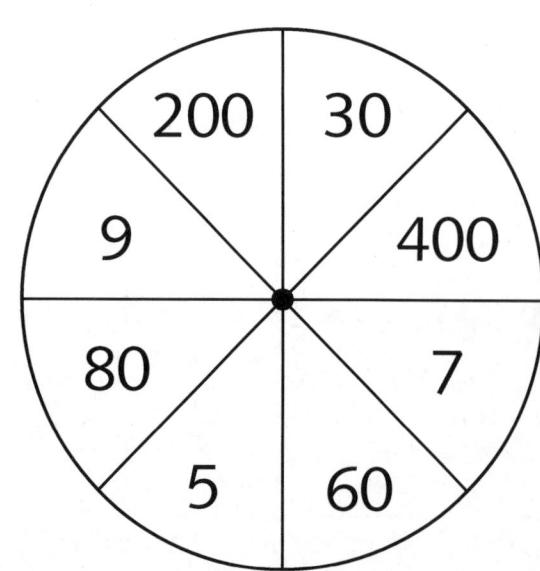

1 [ ] + [ ] = [ ]

2 [ ] + [ ] = [ ]

3 [ ] + [ ] = [ ]

4 [ ] + [ ] = [ ]

5 [ ] + [ ] = [ ]

6 [ ] + [ ] = [ ]

7 [ ] + [ ] = [ ]

8 [ ] + [ ] = [ ]

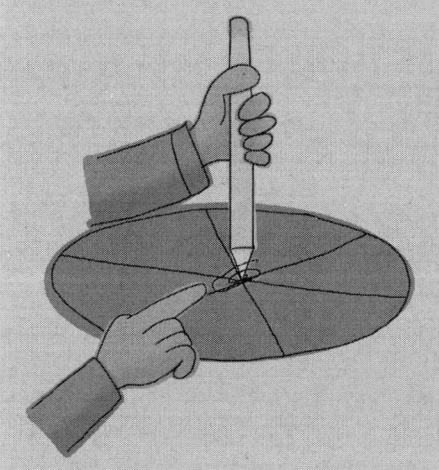

Spinner: 200 | 30 | 400 | 7 | 60 | 5 | 80 | 9

Ask someone at home to make up four addition calculations similar
to those on this sheet and work them out. Check the answers.

Name: _____ Date: _____

Practising the column method for subtraction

Subtract 3-digit numbers using the formal written method of column subtraction

Work out the answers to the calculations using the written method for subtraction. Show your working below.

Challenge 1

a 264 – 132   b 285 – 153   c 374 – 142   d 353 – 122

e 297 – 143   f 385 – 263   g 348 – 126   h 377 – 235

Challenge 2

a 362 – 127   b 475 – 269   c 392 – 165   d 481 – 258

e 543 – 318   f 594 – 267   g 488 – 139   h 516 – 308

Challenge 3

a 647 – 263   b 546 – 318   c 528 – 256   d 684 – 391

e 735 – 428   f 784 – 536   g 876 – 238   h 827 – 654

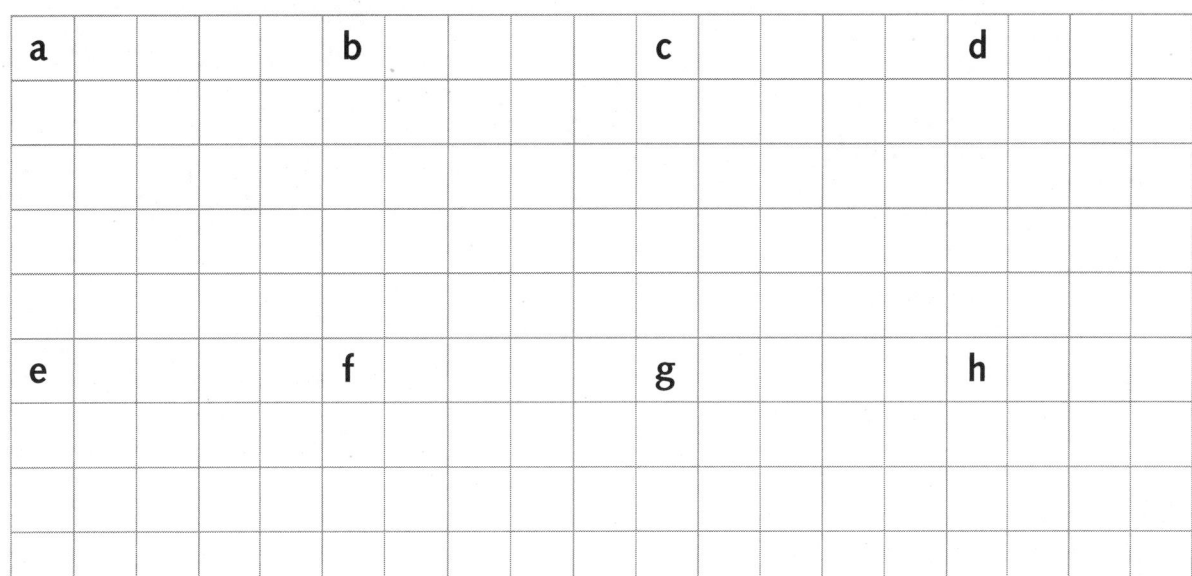

 Choose four of your calculations. Ask someone at home to work them out. Did you both get the same answers?

Name: _____ Date: _____

Spinning subtraction

Subtract numbers mentally and use
inverse operations to check the answer

You will need:
- paper clip and pencil
  – for the spinner

Challenge 1
Choose a first number between 300 and 400.

Challenge 2
Choose a first number between 400 and 600.

Challenge 3
Choose a first number between 600 and 900.

How to use the spinner
Hold the paper clip
in the centre of the
spinner using the pencil
and gently flick the
paper clip with your
finger to make it spin.

- Choose a number to write in the first box
  of the subtraction calculations below.

- Spin the spinner and write the number
  in the second box.

- Work out the calculation, either mentally
  or using a number line.

1 [   ] – [   ] = [   ]

2 [   ] – [   ] = [   ]

3 [   ] – [   ] = [   ]

4 [   ] – [   ] = [   ]

5 [   ] – [   ] = [   ]

6 [   ] – [   ] = [   ]

7 [   ] – [   ] = [   ]

8 [   ] – [   ] = [   ]

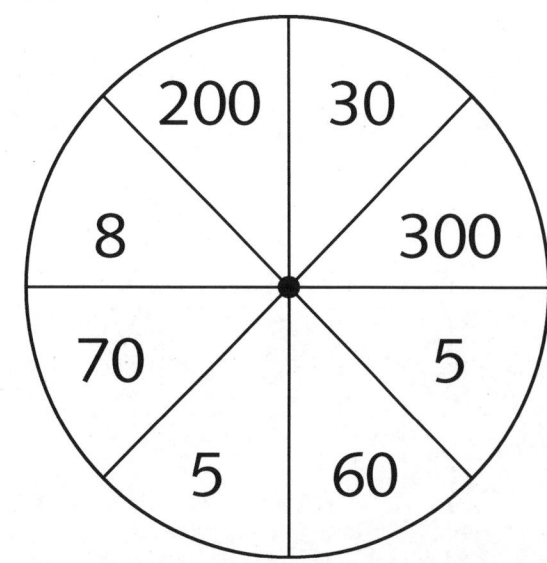

Spinner: 200 | 30 | 300 | 5 | 60 | 5 | 70 | 8

Ask someone at home to make up four subtraction calculations
similar to those on this sheet and work them out. Check the answers.

Name: _____ Date: _____

Keeping a tally

Interpret and present data using tables and charts

Challenges 1,2,3

Count the tally marks. Write the totals in the Frequency column.

Popular words	Tally	Frequency
the	ⅢⅢ ⅢⅢ ⅢⅢ |||	
was	ⅢⅢ ⅢⅢ		
and	ⅢⅢ ⅢⅢ ⅢⅢ ⅢⅢ	
to	ⅢⅢ ⅢⅢ ||	
from	ⅢⅢ ||	
they	ⅢⅢ ⅢⅢ |||	

Challenges 2,3

1 Choose a page from your reading book.

2 Look for these words on the page.
Complete the tally chart.

Popular words	Tally	Frequency
the		
was		
and		
to		
from		
they		

Challenge 3

How is your chart similar to or different from the chart above?

_____

Find an article in a newspaper, magazine, holiday brochure or online.
Predict the six most popular words that the article will contain.
Draw a tally chart on the back of this sheet and complete it.

Name: _____ Date: _____

Tins, packets and bags

Interpret and present data in bar charts
with intervals labelled in multiples of 2

You will need:
- pencil
- paper

Challenges
1, 2, 3

1 Count the number of tins, packets and bags.

Complete the table.

Item	Number
tins	
packets	
bags	

2 a There are more

_____ than tins.

b There are ☐ fewer

bags than tins.

Challenges
2, 3

1 Complete the bar chart
for the above data.

2 Using another sheet of
paper, draw a pictogram
of the data in the bar chart.

Challenge
3

Write three statements about
the data in the bar chart
on the back of this sheet.

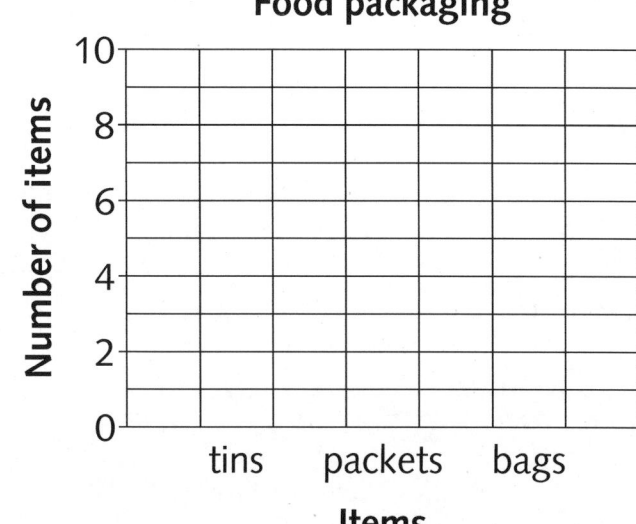

Food packaging

Number of items (y-axis: 0, 2, 4, 6, 8, 10)

Items (x-axis: tins, packets, bags)

Look at the way the food in your cupboards and fridge is packaged.
Count the tins, packets, bags and trays and list them in a table on the
back of this sheet. Ask each other questions which begin with, "How
many more…?" and "How many fewer…?"

Name: _____ Date: _____

Revising multiplication facts

Consolidate recall of the multiplication facts for the 2, 3, 4, 5, 8 and 10 multiplication tables, and related facts involving multiples of 10

Challenge 1

Multiply the middle number with the number on each petal.

1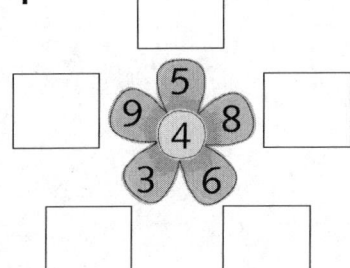

2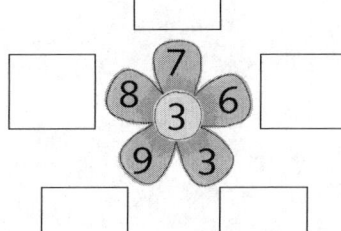

3

Challenge 2

Write two multiplication facts for each of these arrays.

1

2

3

Challenge 3

Complete the table.

x	2	3	4	5	8	10
7						
3			12			
9						
11				55		
60						

 Make your own set of 1–12 number cards. Shuffle the cards and place them face down on the table. Choose a number to multiply: 2, 3, 4, 5, 8 or 10. Take turns to turn over a card and multiply the number on the card by your chosen number. The first player to call out the correct answer keeps the card. The winner is the player with more cards once all 12 cards have been used.

Name: _____ Date: _____

Revising division facts

Consolidate recall of the division facts for
the 2, 3, 4, 5, 8 and 10 multiplication tables

Challenge 1

Cross out the number in each row that is not in the division family of
numbers. Then write two division facts for each set of numbers.

Example

① 8   ✕✕   ① 5   ① 40 | $40 \div 8 = 5$ | $40 \div 5 = 8$ |

| (8) | (33̸) | (5) | (40) | $40 \div 8 = 5$ | $40 \div 5 = 8$ |

(6)	(8)	(48)	(24)		
(7)	(42)	(28)	(4)		
(9)	(72)	(8)	(63)		

Challenge 2

Write two division facts for each of these arrays.

1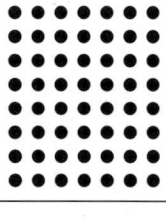

2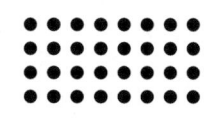

3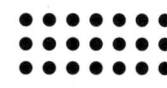

Challenge 3

Divide each set of numbers by the number at the top of each table.

1   ÷4   2   ÷3   3   ÷8

÷4	
28	
48	
32	
360	
200	

÷3	
18	
24	
27	
90	
210	

÷8	
56	
48	
32	
400	
720	

Name: _____ Date: _____

Making pizzas

Compare fractions with the same denominator

You will need:
• coloured pencils

 pepperoni   mushroom   tuna

Make four different pizzas by drawing two toppings on to each pizza.

Rule: You can only use one topping per slice of pizza.

Write two things about the fractions on your pizzas.

 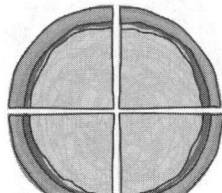 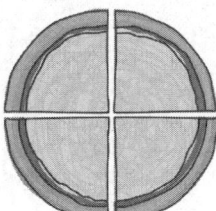 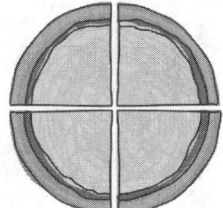

1 _____

2 _____

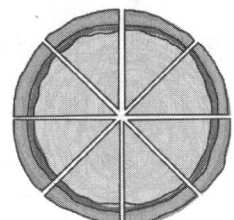  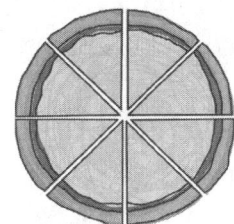 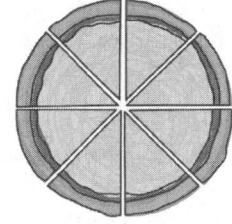

1 _____

2 _____

 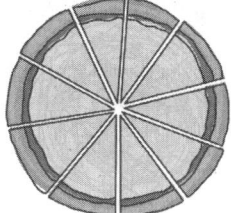 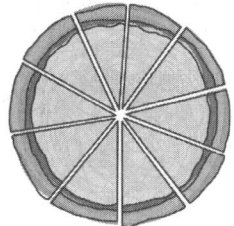 

1 _____

2 _____

 Ask someone at home to create a pizza. They can choose two toppings.
Remember to use only one topping per slice.

Name: _____ **Date:** _____

Fraction snakes

Find equivalent fractions

You will need:
- 1–6 dice
- 2 coloured pencils

Challenges 1, 2

Play this game with a partner.

In this game, your aim is to make snakes that are half one colour and half another colour. They can be horizontal or vertical.

- Take turns to:
  - roll the dice
  - colour in that number of squares on the grid in one colour, then again in the second colour.

- When you complete a snake that is half one colour and half another colour, write your initial on it.

- Your score is the number of squares in half of your snake.

- Play for 15 minutes. Who has the most points?

Make as many half snakes as you can.

I am a halves snake

Challenge 2

Write the fraction for each of your snakes.

Challenge 3

Play the game as described above but make quarter snakes not halves.

I am a quarters snake

 Show your fraction snakes to someone at home. Tell them about the fractions in your snakes.

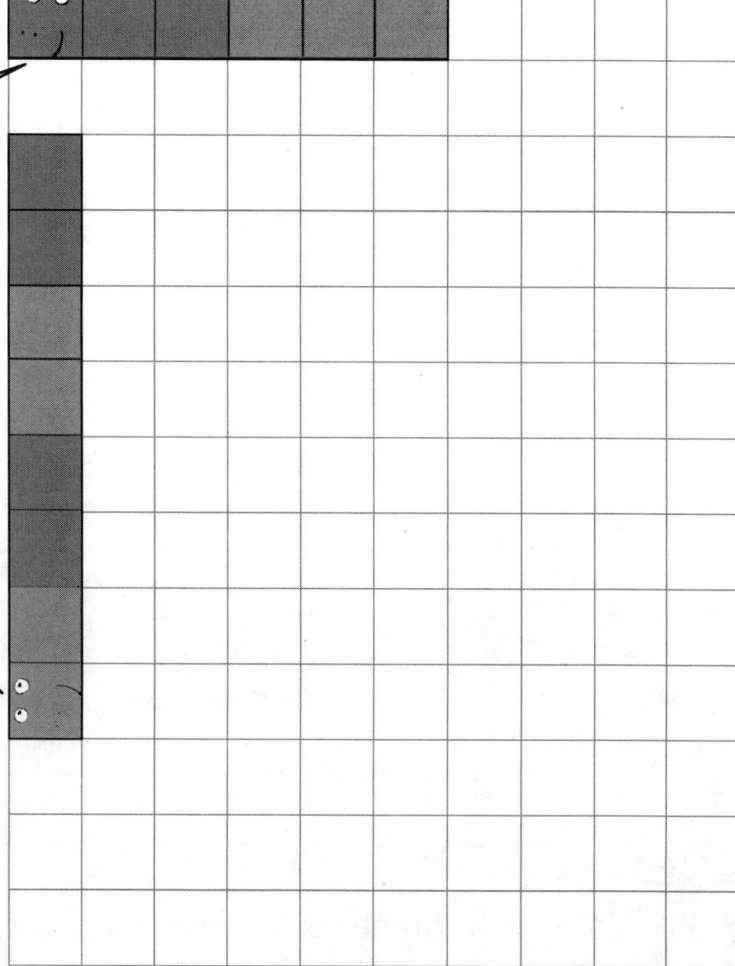

Name: _____ Date: _____

Perimeter search

Measure and calculate the perimeter of regular 2-D shapes

Challenge 1

These shapes are made by fitting together five equilateral triangles.

The dots are 1 cm apart. Find the perimeter of each shape.

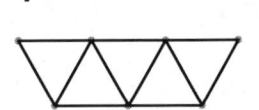

1   P = [ ] cm   2   P = [ ] cm   3   P = [ ] cm   4   P = [ ] cm

Challenge 2

These shapes are made by fitting together six equilateral triangles. Find the perimeter for each shape.

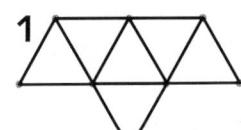 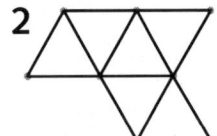 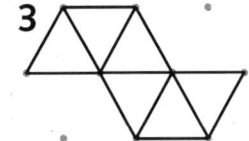 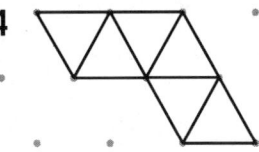

1   P = [ ] cm   2   P = [ ] cm   3   P = [ ] cm   4   P = [ ] cm

Challenge 3

Draw three more shapes you can make using six equilateral triangles and find their perimeters.

Work together to measure the perimeter of different rectangular-shaped objects in the home, for example, place mat, magazine cover, book cover, envelope. Write your results on the back of this sheet.

Name: _____ Date: _____

Join up the rectangles

Measure and calculate the perimeter of 2-D shapes

You will need:
- scissors

Cut out the rectangles below, then use them to find the perimeters.

Challenges 1,2

Make rectangles by joining:

a 1 and 3   perimeter = ☐ cm   **b** 2 and 5   perimeter = ☐ cm

c 3 and 4   perimeter = ☐ cm   **d** 5 and 6   perimeter = ☐ cm

e 4 and 5   perimeter = ☐ cm   **f** 2 and 6   perimeter = ☐ cm

g 3 and 5   perimeter = ☐ cm

Challenge 3

Make rectangles by joining:

a 1, 3 and 5
perimeter = ☐ cm

b 3, 4 and 6
perimeter = ☐ cm

c 1, 3 and 6
perimeter = ☐ cm

d 2, 4 and 6
perimeter = ☐ cm

 Together, look at some tiling patterns at home. Identify rectangles made by two or more square tiles and discuss the perimeter made when two rectangles are joined together. Write what you find on the back of this sheet.

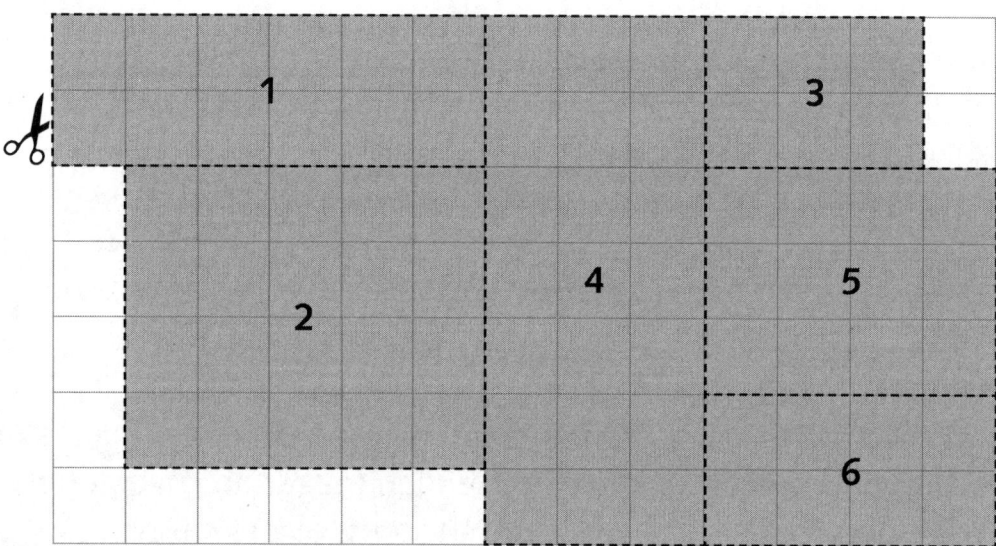

Name: _____ Date: _____

Raffle raffle

Compare and order numbers to 1000

Challenge 1

Write the raffle ticket numbers that come before and after these tickets.

a [ ] | 54 | [ ]   b [ ] | 66 | [ ]

c [ ] | 106 | [ ]   d [ ] | 125 | [ ]

Challenge 2

Fill in the missing raffle ticket numbers.

a | 178 | [ ] | [ ] | [ ] | 182 | [ ] | [ ] | [ ]

b | 599 | [ ] | [ ] | [ ] | [ ] | 604 | [ ] | [ ]

c | 768 | [ ] | [ ] | [ ] | [ ] | [ ] | 775

d | 917 | [ ] | [ ] | [ ] | [ ] | 923 | [ ]

Challenge 3

Seven is my lucky number.
I only buy raffle tickets if the digits add up to seven.
So, I would buy 304 because 3 + 0 + 4 = 7. Tell me
six other tickets I can buy. Write the numbers
in order, smallest to largest.

304

[ ] [ ] [ ] [ ] [ ] [ ]

 Play this game with a partner. Cut up ten small pieces of paper, and share them between you. Secretly write a 3-digit number on each piece of paper and place them face down on the table. Take turns to turn over a piece of paper and say the number out loud. Order the numbers, smallest to largest.

You will need:
- paper
- scissors

Name: _____ Date: _____

Secret numbers

Solve number problems

 Play this game with a partner.

- Take turns to:
  - choose a secret number and write it on the back of this sheet
  - give the other player a clue about your number.

- The other player asks questions until they can guess the number.

- Keep a record of how many questions are asked.

- For each round the player who asks the fewest questions scores a point.

- Play 10 rounds. The player with the most points wins!

I'm thinking of a number. It's between 250 and 300.

Is your number odd?

Is it a multiple of 10?

Is the tens digit a four?

Is it greater than 270?

Challenge 1 Choose numbers between 1 and 100.

Challenge 2 Choose numbers between 100 and 400.

Challenge 3 Choose numbers between 500 and 1000.

Write your jottings here about the number you are guessing.

Player One

Player Two

Name: _____ Date: _____

Mental jumps

Add and subtract numbers mentally

- Choose a starting number and write it in the Start box.
- Work out the calculation on the arrow and write the answer in the next box.
- Continue until all boxes are filled in.

Challenge 1

Choose start numbers between 10 and 100.

Challenge 2

Choose start numbers between 100 and 300.

Challenge 3

Choose start numbers between 300 and 400.

1 Start

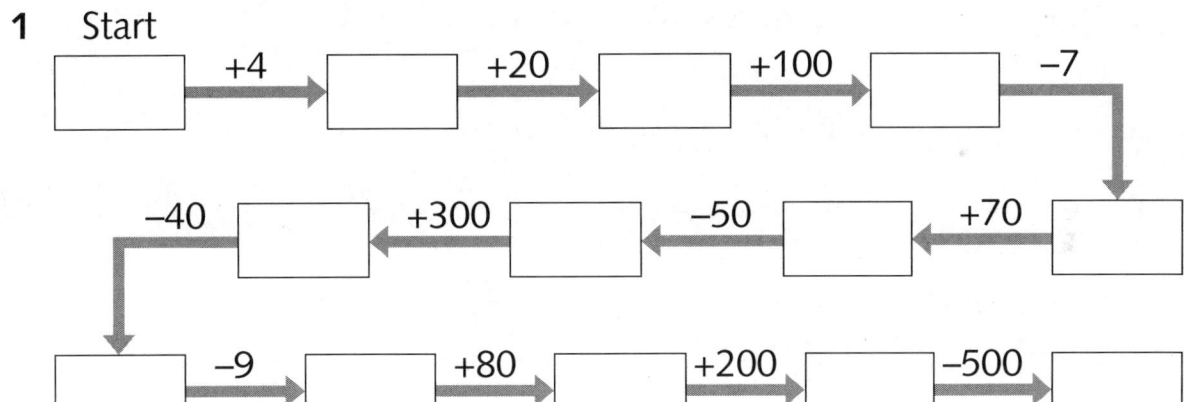

2 Start

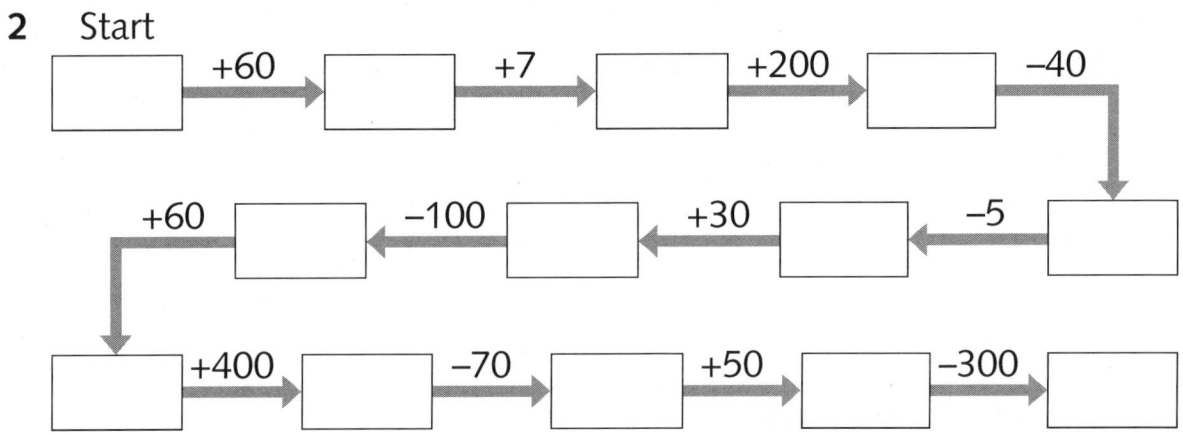

Work with someone at home. Start at the end of the trail and work back, using the inverse operations to check your answers.

Name: _____ **Date:** _____

Practising the column method for subtraction

Subtract 3-digit numbers using the formal written method of column subtraction

Work out the answers to the calculations using the written method for subtraction. Show your working below.

a 363 – 152   **b** 384 – 271   **c** 358 – 126   **d** 395 – 231

e 375 – 112   **f** 348 – 136   **g** 428 – 215   **h** 483 – 262

Challenge 2

a 462 – 217   **b** 473 – 231   **c** 584 – 135   **d** 437 – 119

e 567 – 248   **f** 455 – 129   **g** 548 – 216   **h** 566 – 239

Challenge 3

a 647 – 329   **b** 628 – 254   **c** 617 – 164   **d** 748 – 362

e 752 – 281   **f** 893 – 331   **g** 765 – 282   **h** 877 – 439

a				b				c				d			
e				f				g				h			

 Choose four of your calculations. Ask someone at home to work them out. Did you both get the same answers?

Name: _____ Date: _____

Capital letters

Know when a line is horizontal or vertical

You will need:
- ruler
- blue, red and green pencils

Challenges 1,2,3

1 In each square dot grid, draw a different CAPITAL letter that uses straight lines only. Connect the dots in pencil.

2 Highlight the horizontal lines blue, the vertical lines red and the diagonal lines green.

Challenges 2,3

Write the letters which have:

Set A horizontal and vertical lines only

Set B diagonal lines only

Set C horizontal and diagonal lines

Set D vertical and diagonal lines

Challenge 3

1 Which letter does not belong to Sets **A** to **D**?

2 Describe the letter. _____

_____

On the back of this sheet make a list of objects you find around your home that have horizontal or vertical lines.

Name: _____ Date: _____

Pin board puzzles

Describe the properties of 2-D shapes

You will need:
• ruler

Challenges 1, 2, 3

Read the description above each pin board. Draw the shape on the pin board.

1 4 right angles and opposite sides equal

2 4 sides and 1 angle a right angle

3 4 sides and 2 pairs of parallel lines

Challenges 2, 3

1 3 vertices and 1 angle greater than a right angle

2 4 sides and 1 pair of parallel lines

3 6 sides and 3 pairs of parallel lines

Challenge 3

1 4 equal sides with 2 angles less than a right angle

2 An octagon with opposite sides equal

3 A pentagon with 2 perpendicular sides

On the back of this sheet, draw shapes with 4, 5 and 6 sides. Take turns to describe the properties of each shape.

Name: _____ Date: _____

Multiplication using partitioning

Use partitioning to calculate TO × O

1 9 × 3 = ☐

90 × 3 = ☐

2 3 × 8 = ☐

30 × 8 = ☐

3 6 × 4 = ☐

60 × 4 = ☐

Approximate the answer to each calculation.

Example 63 × 5 → (60 × 5 = 300)

1 54 × 3 → ( )

2 29 × 5 → ( )

3 73 × 4 → ( )

4 92 × 8 → ( )

Partition each of the calculations above to work out the answer. Check your estimate is close to your answer.

Example

63 × 5 = (60 × 5) + (3 × 5)
= 300 + 15
= 315

1 54 × 3 = ☐
= ☐
= ☐

2 29 × 5 = ☐
= ☐
= ☐

3 73 × 4 = ☐
= ☐
= ☐

4 92 × 8 = ☐
= ☐
= ☐

 Choose two calculations. Explain to an adult how you worked them out. Give them two calculations to work out using the same method as you. Check their answers are correct.

Name: _____ Date: _____

Multiplication: Introducing the expanded written method

Use the expanded written method to calculate TO × O

Challenge 1

These calculations are incomplete. Write the missing digits.

a 3 × 9 = 2☐

b 4 × ☐ = 28

c ☐ × 8 = 32

d ☐ × 4 = 16

e 7 × 5 = ☐5

f 6 × ☐ = 24

g 8 × 8 = ☐4

h 6 × ☐ = ☐8

i 1☐ × ☐ = 48

Challenge 2

Approximate the answer to each calculation.

Example 63 × 8 → (60 × 8 = 480)

a 45 × 4 → (   )

b 96 × 5 → (   )

c 37 × 3 → (   )

d 68 × 3 → (   )

Challenge 3

Find the answers to the calculations above using the expanded written method of multiplication. Check your estimate is close to your answer.

You will need:
• squared paper

Example

	H	T	O	
		6	3	
×			8	
		2	4	(3 × 8)
	4	8	0	(60 × 8)
	5	0	4	
	1			

 Choose two calculations. Ask an adult to show you how they would work out the answers to the calculations. Explain to an adult how you worked them out. Discuss how your methods are similar or different.

Name: _____ Date: _____

Home fractions

Solve fraction word problems

Make up some fraction word problems about your family.
You could use some real examples of
things being shared out at home.
Use the back of this sheet if you
need more space.

> I have
> one brother
> so we halve
> lots of things.

Challenge 1

Make up two fraction word problems.

For each problem draw a diagram to show the fractions.

> (empty answer box)

Challenge 2

Make up four fraction word problems.

> (empty answer box)

Challenge 3

Make up four fraction word problems. Try and include more than one
operation in each problem.

> (empty answer box)

 Read two of your word problems to someone at home. Can they work
out the answers? Ask them to tell you about a time when they used
fractions. Write what they tell you on the back of this sheet.

Name: _____ Date: _____

Fraction wall equivalents

Recognise equivalent fractions

You will need:
• coloured pencils

Look at the fraction wall.

1									

$\frac{1}{2}$	$\frac{1}{2}$

$\frac{1}{3}$	$\frac{1}{3}$	$\frac{1}{3}$

$\frac{1}{4}$	$\frac{1}{4}$	$\frac{1}{4}$	$\frac{1}{4}$

$\frac{1}{5}$	$\frac{1}{5}$	$\frac{1}{5}$	$\frac{1}{5}$	$\frac{1}{5}$

$\frac{1}{6}$	$\frac{1}{6}$	$\frac{1}{6}$	$\frac{1}{6}$	$\frac{1}{6}$	$\frac{1}{6}$

$\frac{1}{8}$	$\frac{1}{8}$	$\frac{1}{8}$	$\frac{1}{8}$	$\frac{1}{8}$	$\frac{1}{8}$	$\frac{1}{8}$	$\frac{1}{8}$

$\frac{1}{10}$	$\frac{1}{10}$	$\frac{1}{10}$	$\frac{1}{10}$	$\frac{1}{10}$	$\frac{1}{10}$	$\frac{1}{10}$	$\frac{1}{10}$	$\frac{1}{10}$	$\frac{1}{10}$

Challenge 1

Find and colour four different equivalent fractions.

Challenge 2

Find and colour five different equivalent fractions.

Challenge 3

Write different sets of equivalent fractions on the back of this sheet. Try and make as many as you can.

Show your fraction wall to someone at home. Ask them some fraction questions.

Tell me a fraction that is equivalent to one third.

Name: _____ Date: _____

Multiples of millilitres

- Measure and compare capacities
- Use simple scaling of quantities and equivalents of mixed units

Challenge 1

You have four jugs, 100 ml, 200 ml, 400 ml and 800 ml.
You can make 500 ml by filling the 100 ml and 400 ml jugs.
Tick the jugs you use to make these amounts.

Amount	100 ml	200 ml	400 ml	800 ml
500 ml	✓		✓	
600 ml				
700 ml				
800 ml				

Challenge 2

Find the amount in millilitres when you fill each jug these number of times.

Size of jug	2 times	3 times	5 times
100 ml	200 ml	ml	ml
200 ml	ml	ml	ml
400 ml	ml	ml	ml
800 ml	ml	ml	ml

Challenge 3

Complete the table by using the four jugs in Challenge 1.

Amount	100 ml	200 ml	400 ml	800 ml
900 ml	✓			✓
1100 ml				
1300 ml				
1500 ml				

Find a measuring jug in your kitchen and write how many millilitres it can measure. Use the measuring jug and water to find the capacity of a bucket. Save the water in your bucket and re-use it to find the capacity of a basin and a large saucepan.

You will need:
- measuring jug
- water
- bucket, basin and large saucepan

Name: _____ Date: _____

Kitchen capacities

Add and subtract capacity using mixed units

Challenges
1,2

1 A  550 ml   B 470 ml   C 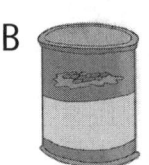 240 ml   D  50 ml

Complete the table. Use the back of this sheet to show your working out.

Container	Measurers used	Capacity in ml
a vase	2 of A + 1 of B	
b jar	1 of B + 2 of C + 1 of D	
c bowl	1 of A + 2 of B + 1 of C	
d pan	3 of A + 3 of D	

2 How many more millilitres does the pan hold than:

  a the vase? ☐   **b** the jar? ☐   **c** the bowl? ☐

Challenge
3

You have three jugs and an empty container.

Use the jugs to fill the empty container to the following amounts using the least amount of steps each time.

 $\frac{1}{4}l$  $\frac{1}{10}l$  600 ml

  a 750 ml   **b** 250 ml

  c 400 ml   **d** 550 ml

  e 50 ml   **f** 1000 ml

Draw a table on the back of this sheet to record your work.

Example

Pour in	Pour out	Leaves
600 ml + $\frac{1}{10}l$	$\frac{1}{4}l$	450 ml

 Work with someone at home to find:

- how many tea cups you can fill from the teapot in your house
- how many mugs of coffee you can make from a full kettle of water.

Name: _____ Date: _____

Meet my addition target

- Add 3-digit numbers using the formal written method of column addition
- Estimate and check the answers to a calculation

You will need:
- 1–6 dice

Roll the dice and fill in the 100s, 10s and 1s digits in the calculations below.

Be thinking how to make your target number.

When the digits are filled in, work out the calculation.

Are you near your total?

Challenge 1

Your target number is 300.

Challenge 2

Your target number is 400.

Challenge 3

Your target number is 600.

1 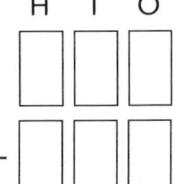   **2** 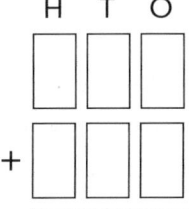   **3** 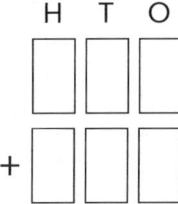   **4**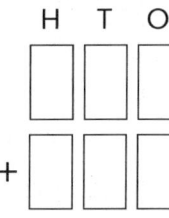

5 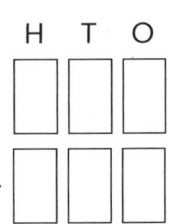   **6** 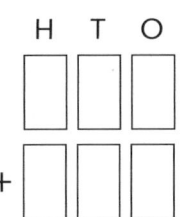   **7** 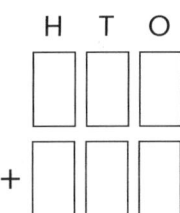   **8**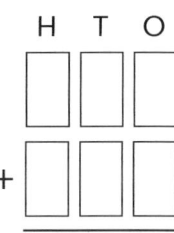

 Ask someone at home to roll the dice and make up a calculation. How close did they get to your target number?

Name: _____ Date: _____

Finding change

Subtract amounts of money

£245

£90

£114

£268

£167

£43

£27

£99

£78

£186

Challenge 1

You have £100 to spend. Work out the change for each item you can afford to buy.

Challenge 2

You have £200 to spend. Work out the change for each item you can afford to buy.

Challenge 3

You have £500 to spend. Work out the change for each item you can afford to buy.

Working out. Also use the back of this sheet if you need to.

 Tell someone at home how much money they have to spend. Ask them to choose an item and work out the change. Did they get it right?

Name: _____ **Date:** _____

Meet my subtraction target

- Subtract 3-digit numbers using the formal written method of column subtraction
- Estimate and check the answers to a calculation

Roll the dice and fill in the 100s, 10s and 1s digits in the calculations below.

Be thinking how to make your target number.

When the digits are filled in, work out the calculation.

Are you near your total?

 **Challenge 1** Your target number is 100.

Challenge 2 Your target number is 200.

Challenge 3 Your target number is 300.

1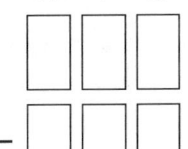

2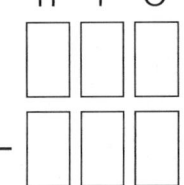

3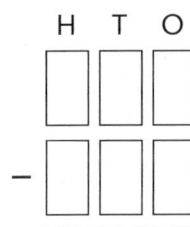

4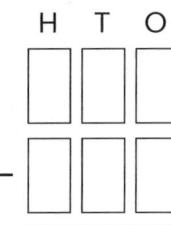

5

6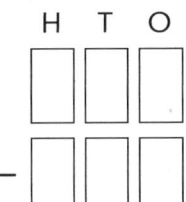

7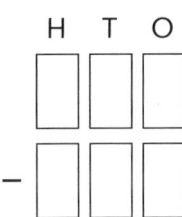

8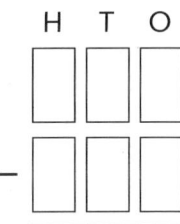

 Ask someone at home to roll the dice and make up a calculation. How close did they get to your target number?

Name: _____ Date: _____

Jumping forwards and backwards

Subtract numbers mentally

For each question:
- write the **circle** number in the circle at the **start** of both number lines
- write the **rectangle** number in the rectangle at the **end** of both number lines
- on the **first** number line, jump **forward** from the smaller number to the larger number
- on the **second** number line, jump **backwards** from the larger number to the smaller number.

 Challenge 1

1 (35) [84]

2 (52) [106]

 Challenge 2

1 (126) [225]

2 (147) [265]

 Challenge 3

1 (356) [457]

2 (392) [513]

1

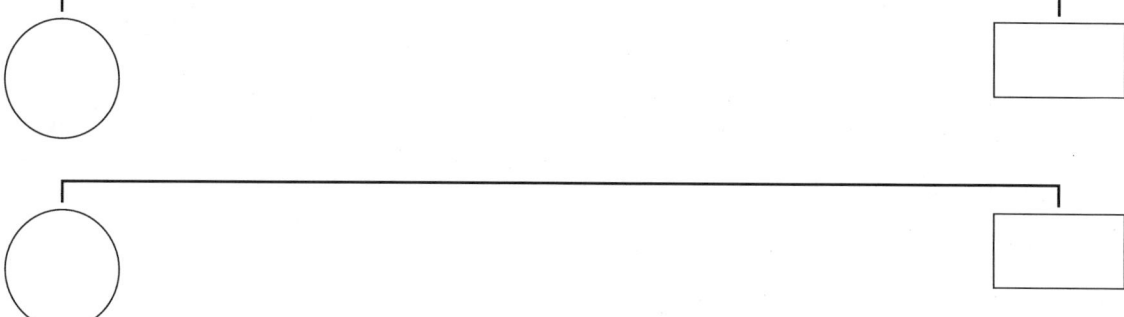

2

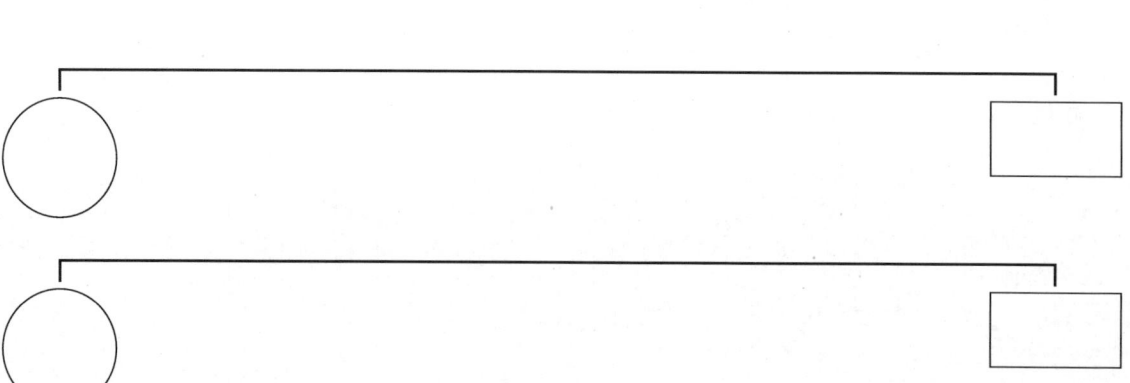

 Tell someone at home the start number, then call out your jumps and ask them to work them out mentally.

Name: _____ Date: _____

Calendar patterns

Know the number of days in each month and year

AUGUST						
M	T	W	Th	F	S	S
			14	15	16	

Challenges 1, 2, 3

The calendar shows that the 14th of August is a Thursday.

Write the numbers for the missing days in the calendar.

Challenges 2, 3

1 a Circle the even dates on your calendar in the first colour.

b Start at 3. Count on in 3s. Circle the numbers you land on in your second colour.

c List the dates which have two circles. _____

You will need:
• 2 coloured pencils

Challenge 3

Describe the patterns you spot:

a for the even numbers

_____

b for the multiples of 3

_____

 Find a copy of this year's calendar. On the back of this sheet write the date and day of the week that all of the members of your family had, or are having, their birthday this year.

Name: _____ Date: _____

Today's TV Guide

Calculate and compare the time taken to complete a task or event

Challenges 1,2,3

Use a copy of today's TV Guide or use the 'Guide' button on the TV handset.

Complete the TV timetable for your favourite channel.

Channel _____	
Time	**Programme**
5:00 p.m.	
5:30 p.m.	
6:00 p.m.	
6:30 p.m.	
7:00 p.m.	
7:30 p.m.	

Challenges 2,3

Choose three programmes from the list opposite and complete the table.

Title of TV programme	Starting time	Finishing time	Length in minutes

Challenge 3

Andy is a fan of cartoons. He watches two half hour programmes of cartoons every day.

How many hours of cartoons could he watch:

a in one week? [ ]   **b** in July? [ ]

Ask an adult what their favourite TV programme is and how often they watch it in one week. Working together, calculate the length of the programme in minutes. Then calculate, in hours and minutes, the time they spend watching it in one week.

Record your answers on the back of this sheet.

Name: _____ Date: _____

Multiplication: Introducing the formal written method

Use the formal written method to calculate TO × O

Challenge 1

Round each of these numbers to the nearest multiple of 10.

a 62 [ ]   b 78 [ ]   c 34 [ ]

d 81 [ ]   e 55 [ ]   f 97 [ ]

Challenge 2

Approximate the answer to each calculation.

Example

$68 \times 3 \rightarrow$ ($70 \times 3 = 210$)

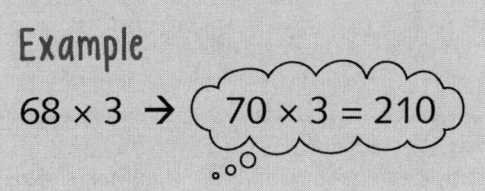

a $45 \times 4 \rightarrow$ ( )   b $96 \times 5 \rightarrow$ ( )

c $37 \times 3 \rightarrow$ ( )   d $84 \times 8 \rightarrow$ ( )

e $68 \times 3 \rightarrow$ ( )   f $76 \times 5 \rightarrow$ ( )

Challenge 3

On squared paper find the answers to the calculations above using the formal written method of multiplication. Check your estimate is close to your answer.

You will need:
- squared paper

Example

H	T	O
	6	8
×	2	3
2	0	4

Choose two calculations and show an adult how you worked them out.

Name: _____ Date: _____

Solving problems

Use the formal written method to calculate TO × O

Challenge 1

1   8

   5

   7

   3

2   4

   9

   7

   3

Challenge 2

Answer these word problems on the back of this sheet.

1 Each bus holds 58 people. How many people can fit in 4 buses?

2 A pencil pot holds 49 pencils. How many pencils are in 8 pencil pots?

3 A jar holds 56 biscuits. A packet holds 38 biscuits. How many more biscuits does the jar hold?

4 Tricycles have 3 wheels. How many wheels are there altogether if there are 67 tricycles?

5 There are 82 cakes and 5 children. Each child eats one cake. How many cakes are left?

6 Mary arranges 78 bunches of flowers. Each bunch has 5 flowers in it. How many flowers are there altogether?

Challenge 3

On the back of this sheet write a word problem for each of these calculations:

1 47 × 4 =   2 73 × 8 =

 Show two of the word problems to an adult and ask them to solve and then explain how they worked them out. Check to see if their answer is correct by showing them how you would work it out.

Name: _____ Date: _____

Division using partitioning

Use partitioning to calculate TO ÷ O

Challenge 1

Find and colour the multiples of 4, 8 and 3.

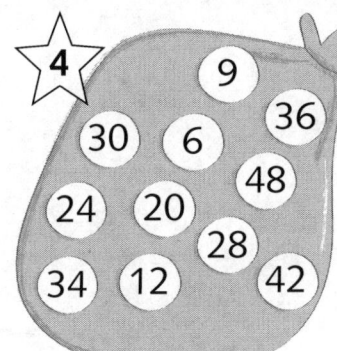
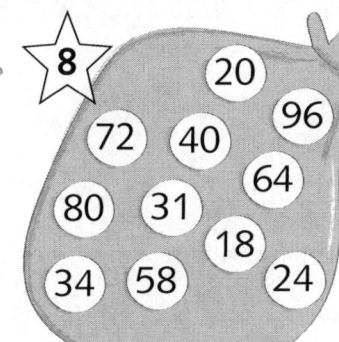
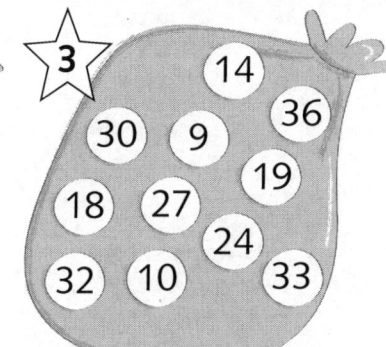

Challenge 2

Approximate the answer to each calculation.

Example

69 ÷ 3 → (60 ÷ 3 = 20)

1 86 ÷ 2 →

2 48 ÷ 4 →

3 88 ÷ 4 →

4 96 ÷ 3 →

Challenge 3

Partition each of the numbers in Challenge 2 to help you find the answer to the division calculation. Show your working on the back of this sheet. Check your answer is close to your estimate.

Example

69 ÷ 3 = (60 + 9) ÷ 3
= 20 + 3
= 23

1 86 ÷ 2 = ☐

2 48 ÷ 4 = ☐

3 88 ÷ 4 = ☐

4 96 ÷ 3 = ☐

 Look for things at home or out shopping that are divided or packaged into groups. Draw or write about them on the back of this sheet.

Name: _____ Date: _____

Division using the formal written method

Use the formal written method to calculate TO ÷ O

Challenge 1

1 16 ÷ 4 = ☐

160 ÷ 4 = ☐

2 32 ÷ 8 = ☐

320 ÷ 8 = ☐

3 24 ÷ 4 = ☐

240 ÷ 4 = ☐

4 21 ÷ 3 = ☐

210 ÷ 3 = ☐

5 35 ÷ 5 = ☐

350 ÷ 5 = ☐

6 16 ÷ 8 = ☐

160 ÷ 8 = ☐

Challenge 2

1 Choose two numbers from the number cards.
Divide each number by 3. Estimate the answer
first then use the formal written method.

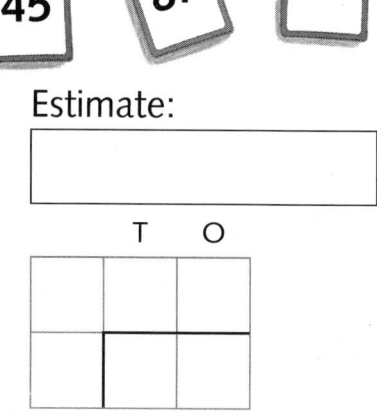

Example

Estimate:

| 72 ÷ 3 → 20 |

	T	O
	2	4
3	7	¹2

Estimate:

| | | |

	T	O

Estimate:

| | | |

	T	O

2 Choose two numbers from the number cards below. Divide each number
by 4. Estimate the answer first then use the formal written method.

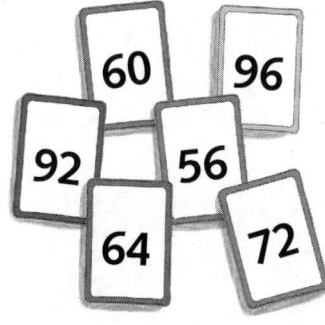

Estimate:

| | | |

	T	O

Estimate:

| | | |

	T	O

Challenge 3

On the back of this sheet write three TO ÷ O division calculations that
have an answer of 19.

 Choose two of the calculations above. Show an adult how you worked
them out using the formal written method of division.

Name: _____ Date: _____

Weather pictograms

Show data in a pictogram where a picture represents 2 units

Year 3 at Craigdhu School made this table for the number of rainy or sunny days from March to July.

Weather	March	April	May	June	July
Rainy	10	12	8	4	6
Sunny	12	16	10	20	14

Challenges 1,2,3

Complete the pictogram.

Rainy days

March					
April					
May					
June					
July					

Key:
🌢 = 2 rainy days

Challenges 2,3

Complete the pictogram.

Sunny days

March					
April					
May					
June					
July					

Key:
☀ = 4 sunny days
◖ = 2 sunny days

Challenge 3

The remaining days of each month were cloudy. Work out how many days were cloudy. Write your answers on the back of this sheet.

Find out from the internet, TV or a newspaper, the Weather Forecast Maps for your weather for the next five days.

Make a table to record the number of symbols for sun, rain and clouds shown on the map each day, for five days. Record your results on the back of this sheet.

Name: _____ Date: _____

Coins bar chart

Answer questions about data in scaled bar charts and tables

Challenges 1, 2, 3

1 Ask someone at home to put 1 or 2 of each 1p, 2p, 5p and 10p coins in a bag. Take a coin from the bag, record it in the tally chart and return it to the bag. Do this 20 times.

Coin	Tally	Total
1p		
2p		
5p		
10p		

You will need:
- 2 × 1p, 2 × 2p, 2 × 5p and 2 × 10p coins
- bag

2 Complete the Total column of the chart.

Challenges 2, 3

1 a Calculate the total value for each coin from the tally chart above.

   b Complete the table below.

Coin	Value in pence
1p	
2p	
5p	
10p	

2 Complete the bar chart. Choose a suitable scale for the vertical axis.

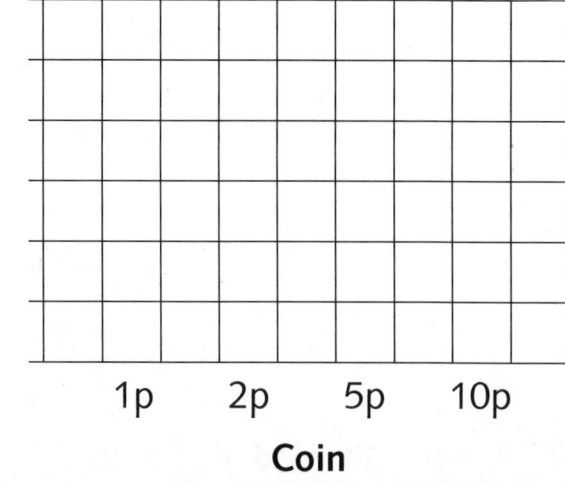

Value of coins taken from bag

Value of coins (pence) — 1p, 2p, 5p, 10p — Coin

Challenge 3

Using each word only once, write five statements about the bar chart on the back of this sheet.

fewer   more than
least often   difference   less

Take turns asking each other questions about the information presented in the tally chart and/or bar chart. Record two of the questions and their answers on the back of this sheet.